MANDALAS

AND FLOWER DOODLE DESIGNS

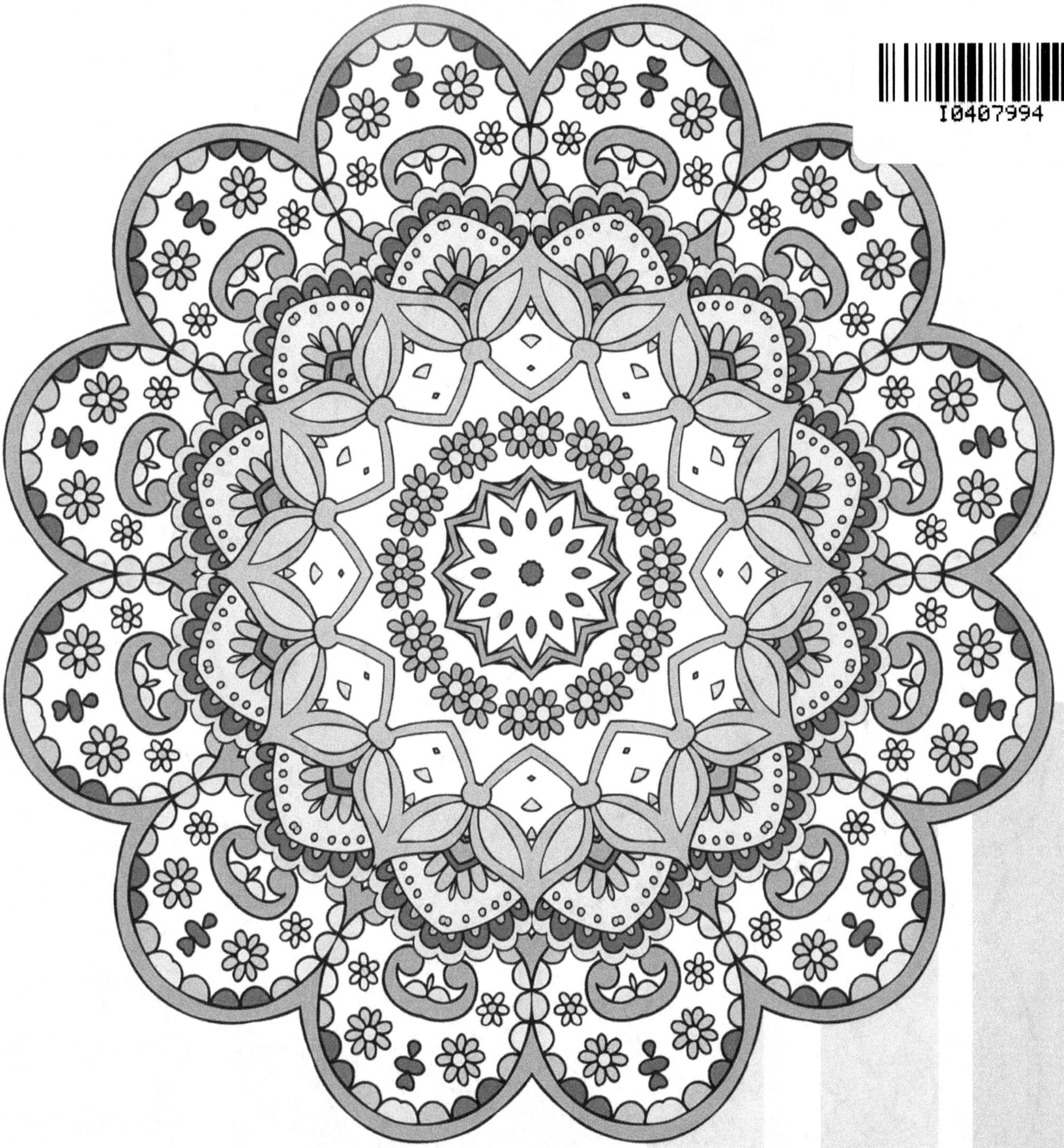

ADULT COLORING BOOK

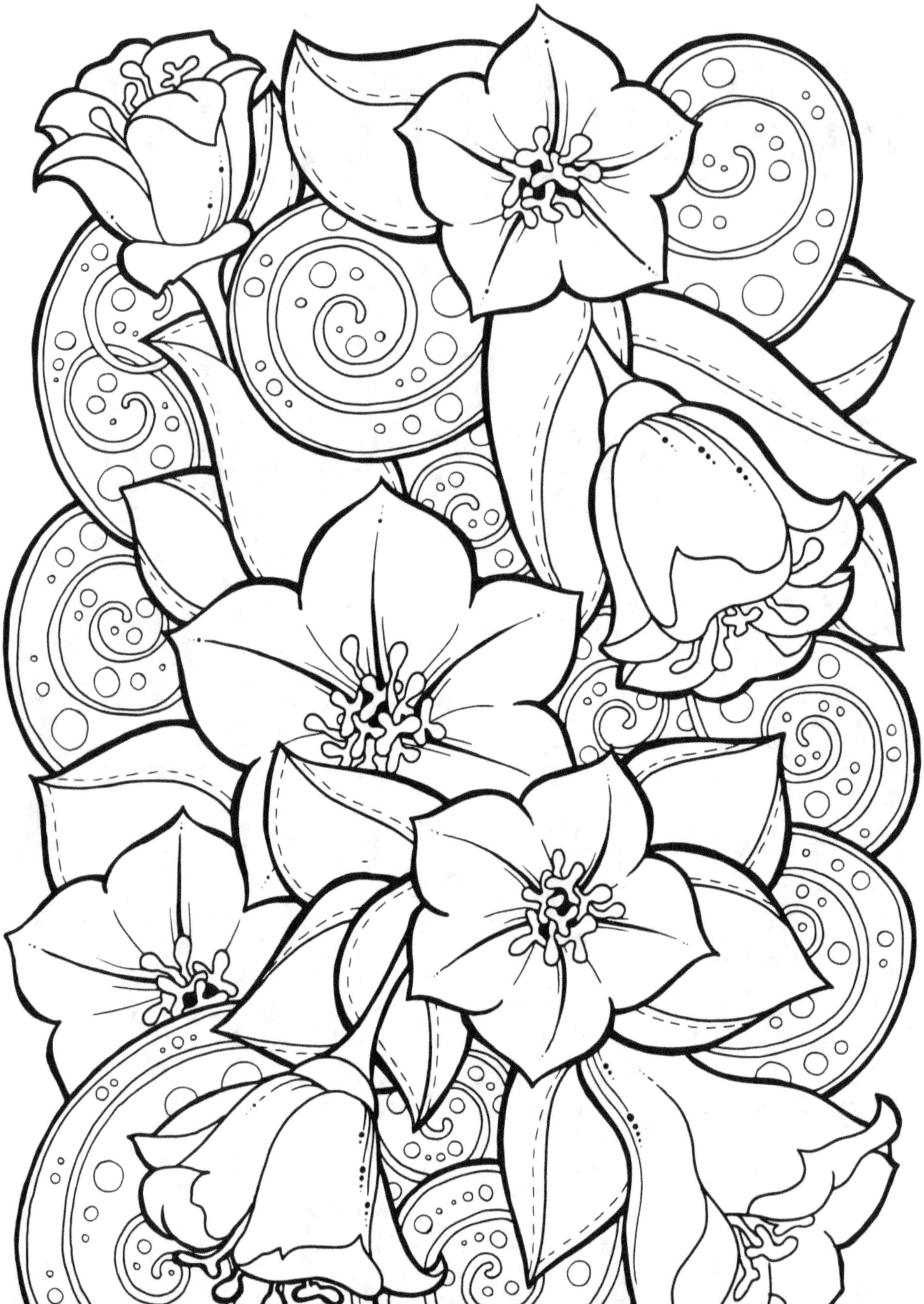

TEST YOUR COLOR

TEST YOUR COLOR

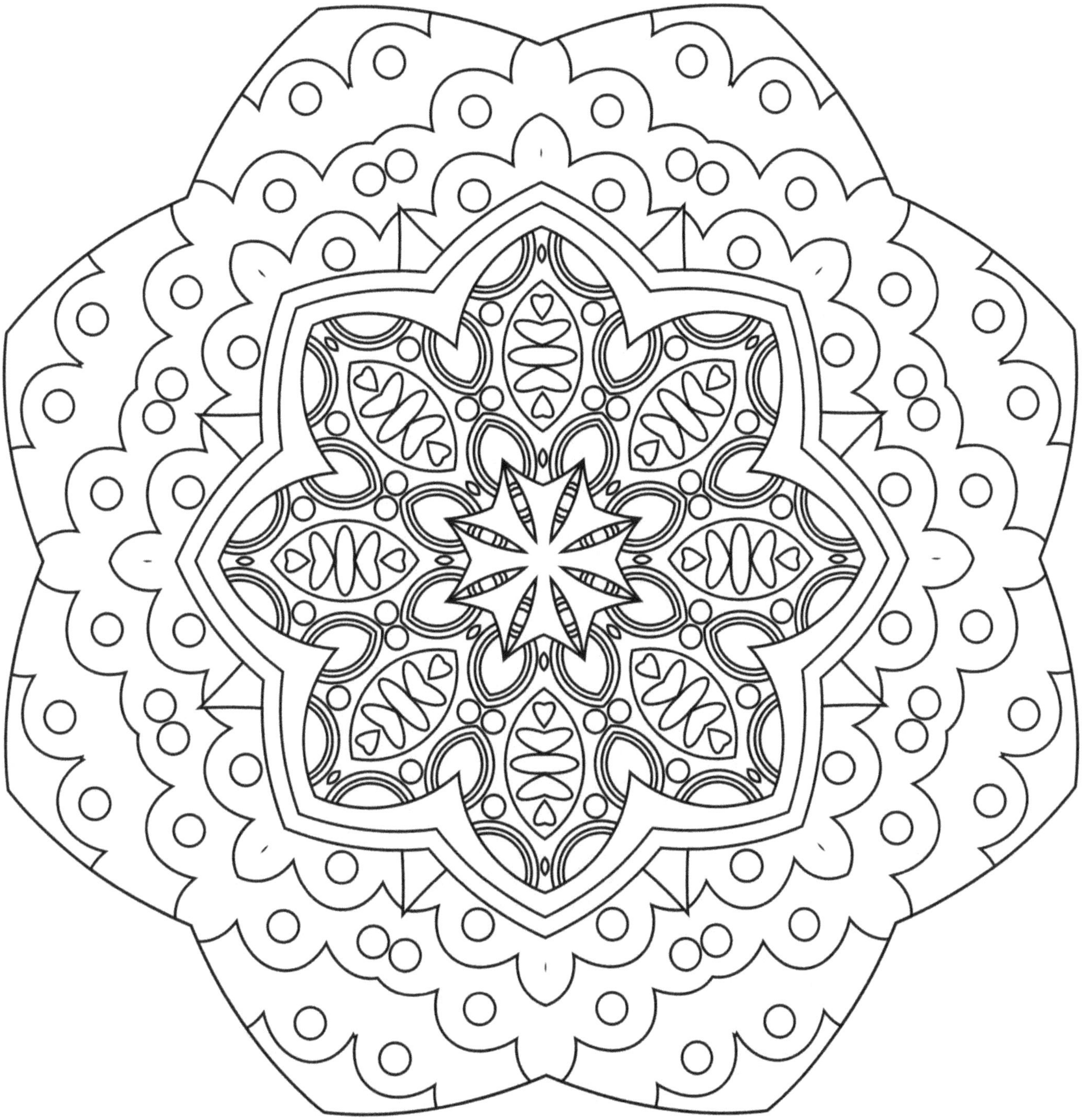

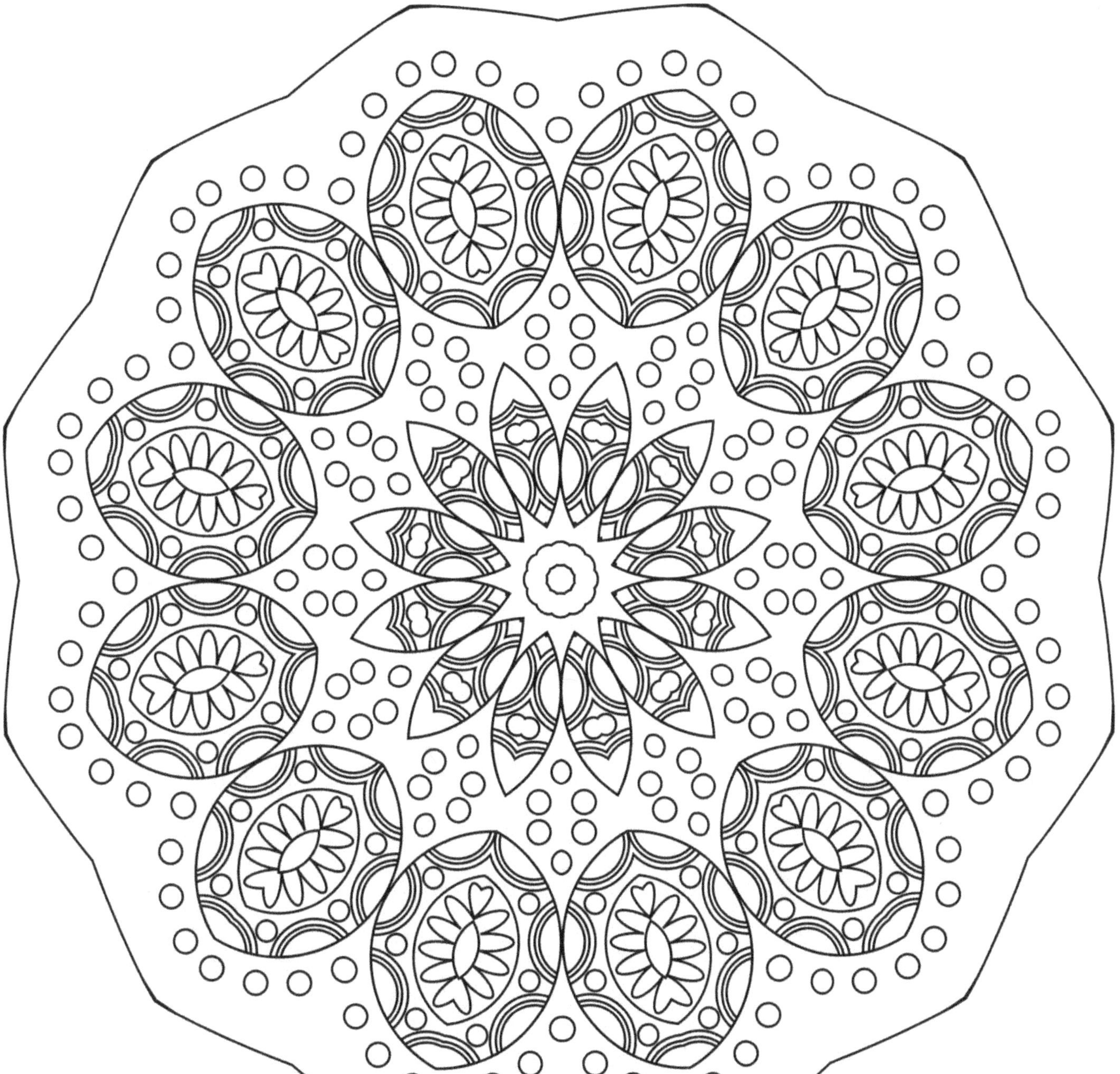

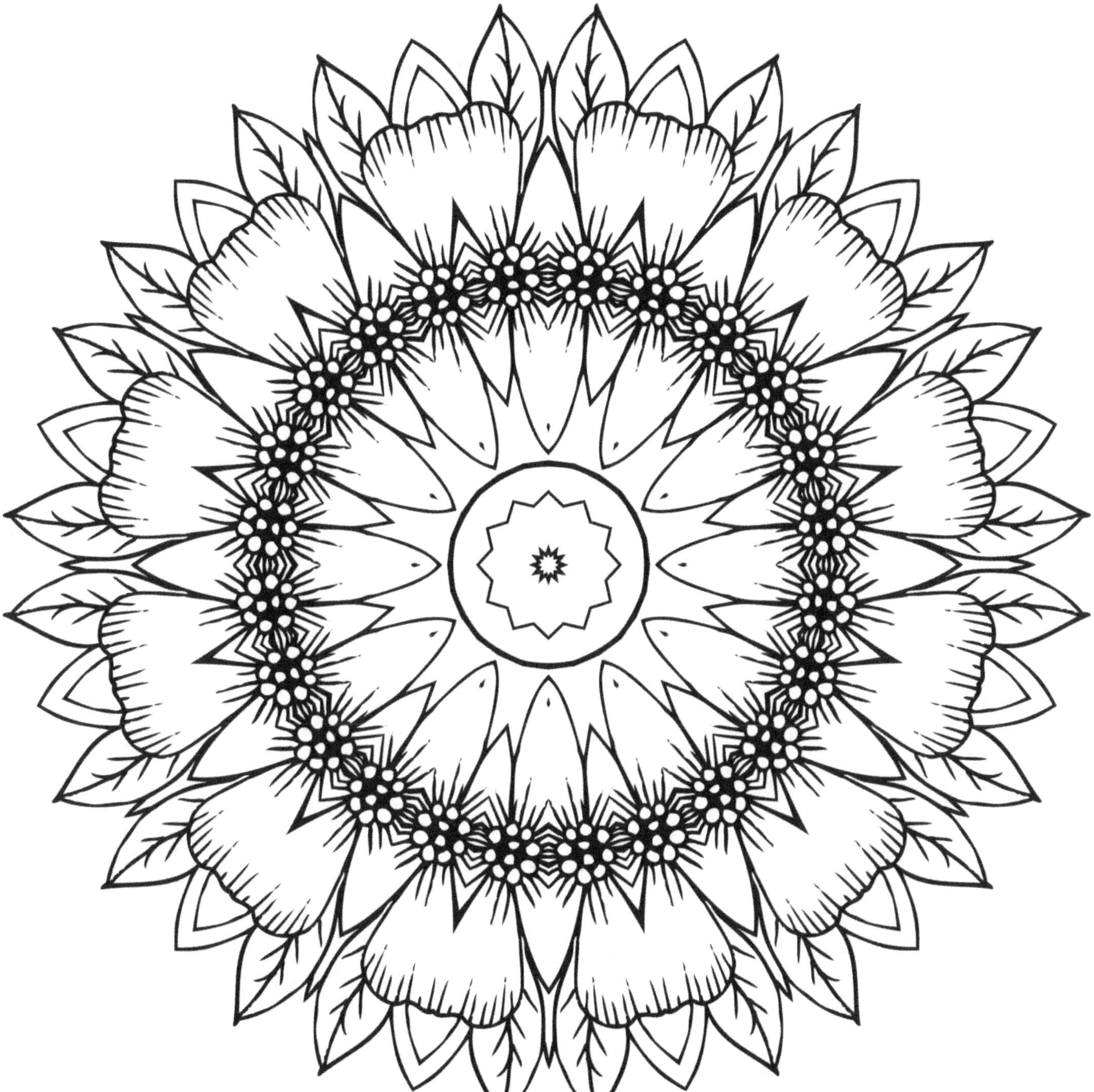

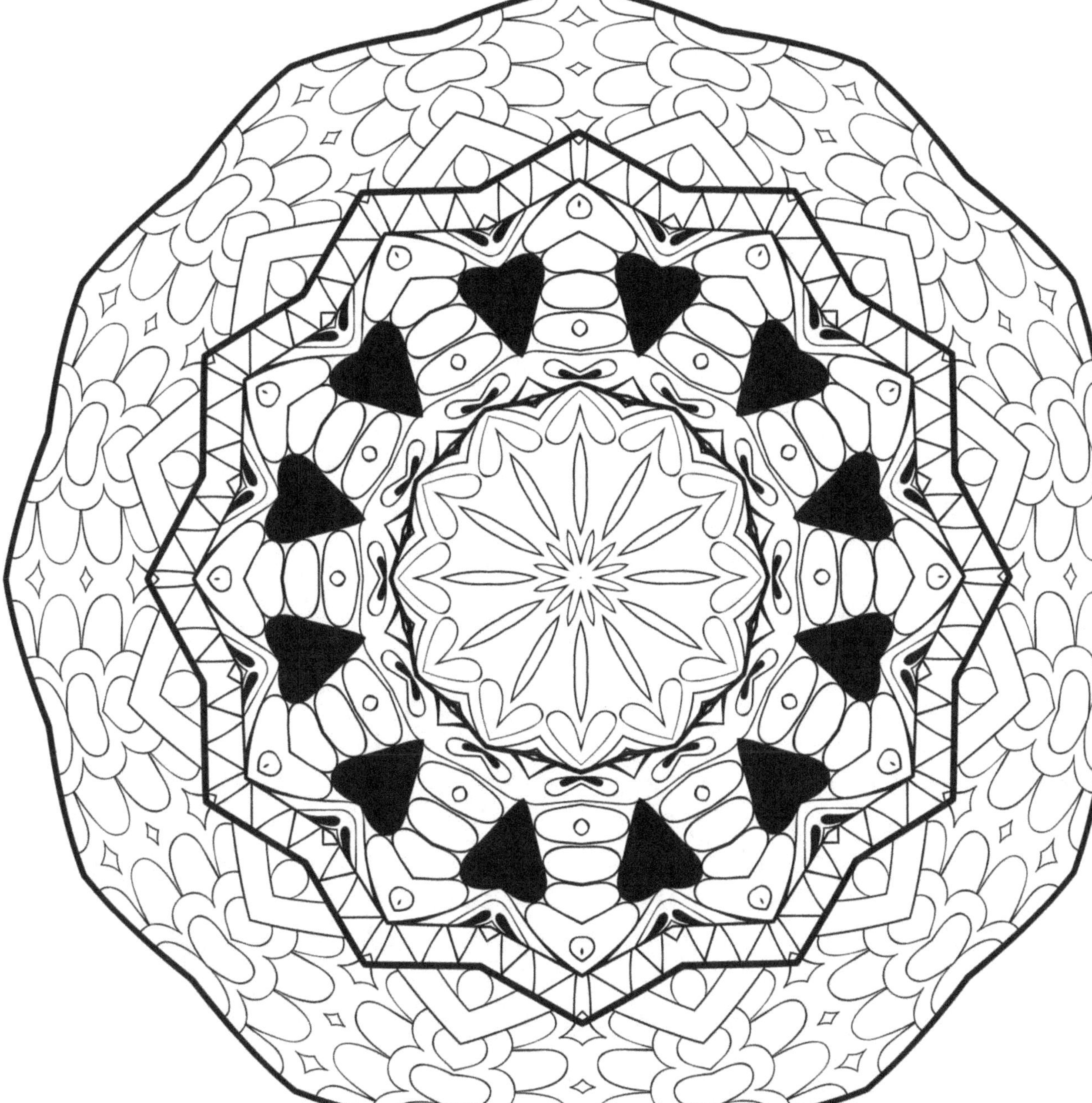

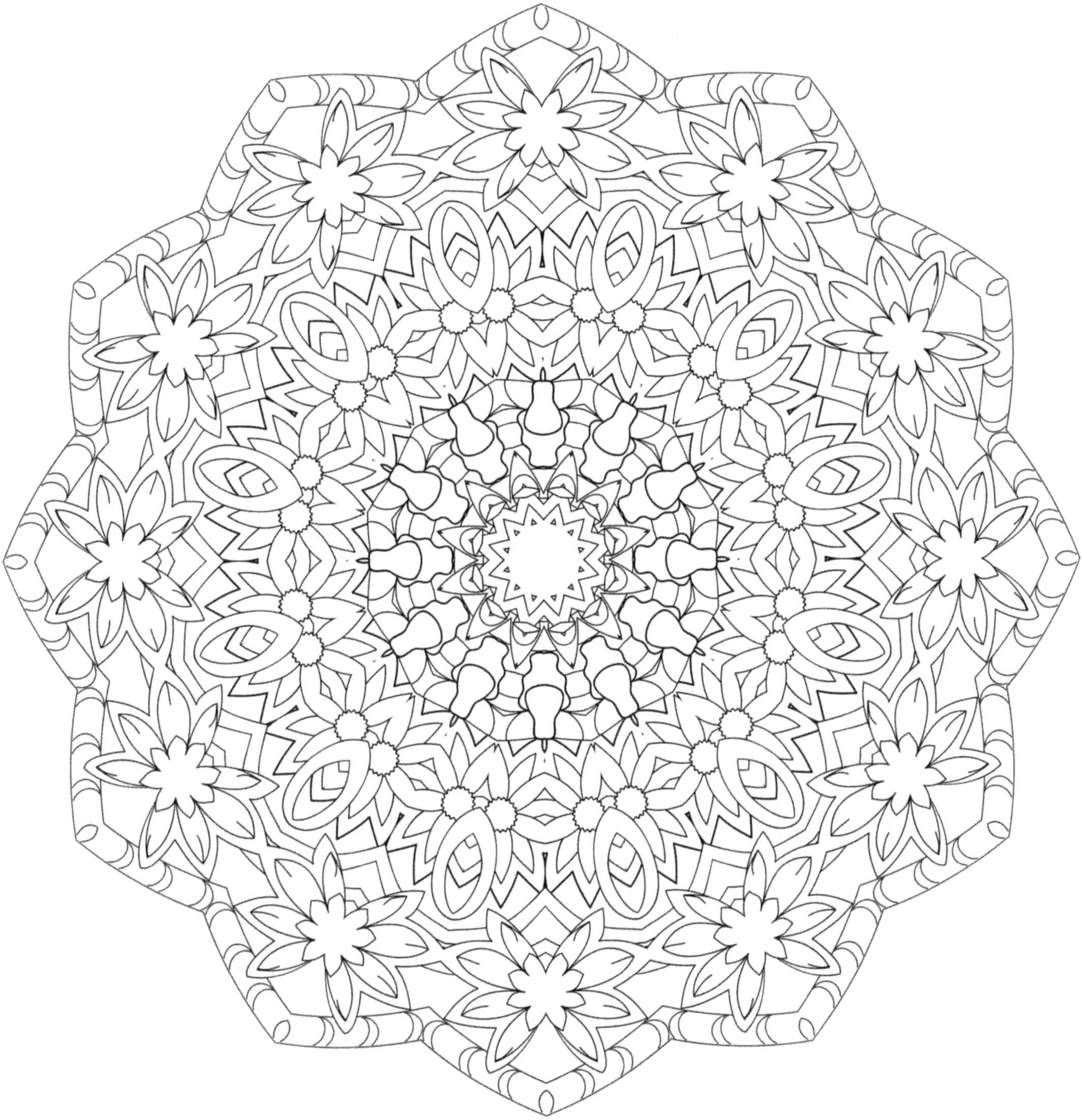

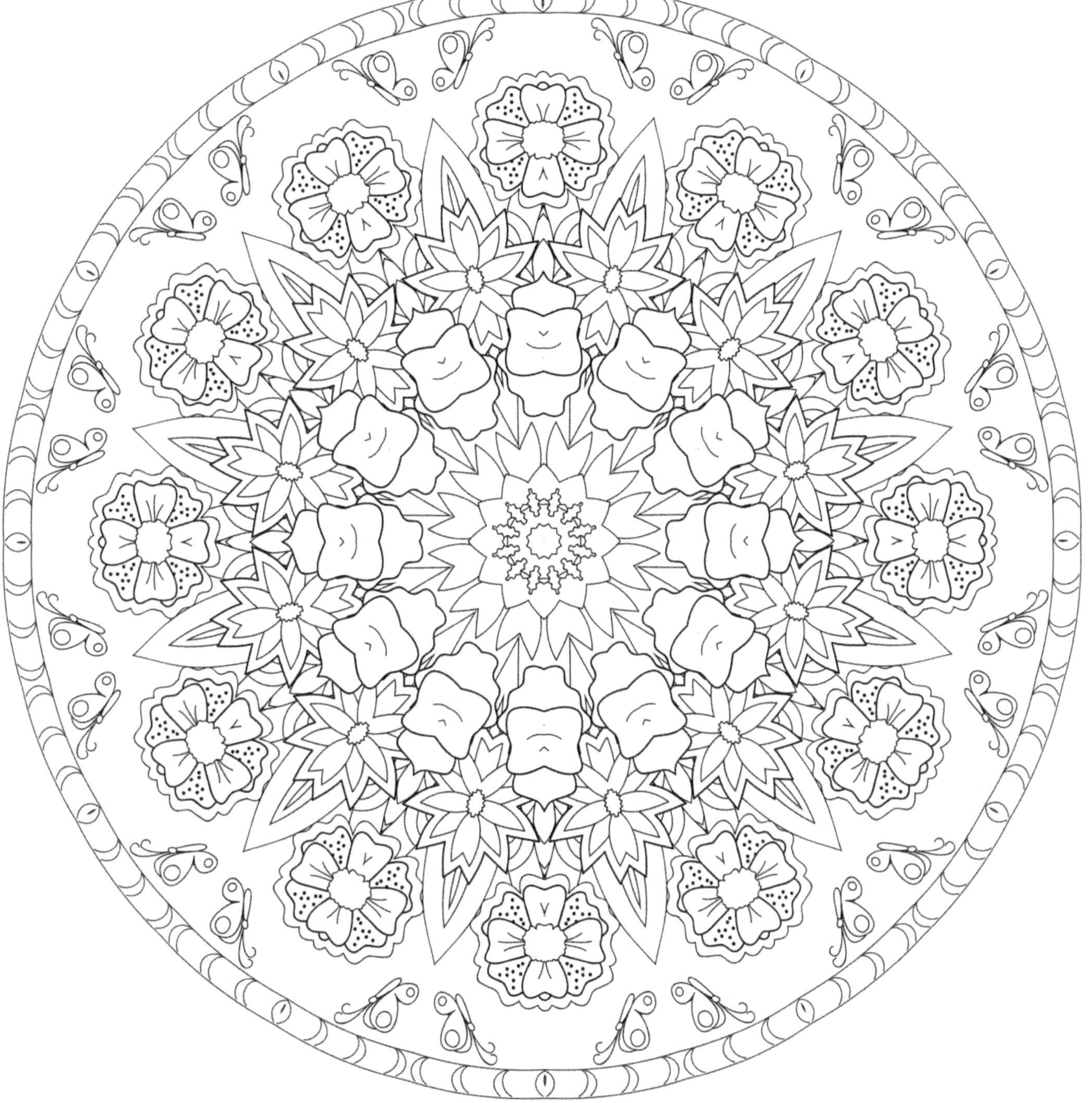

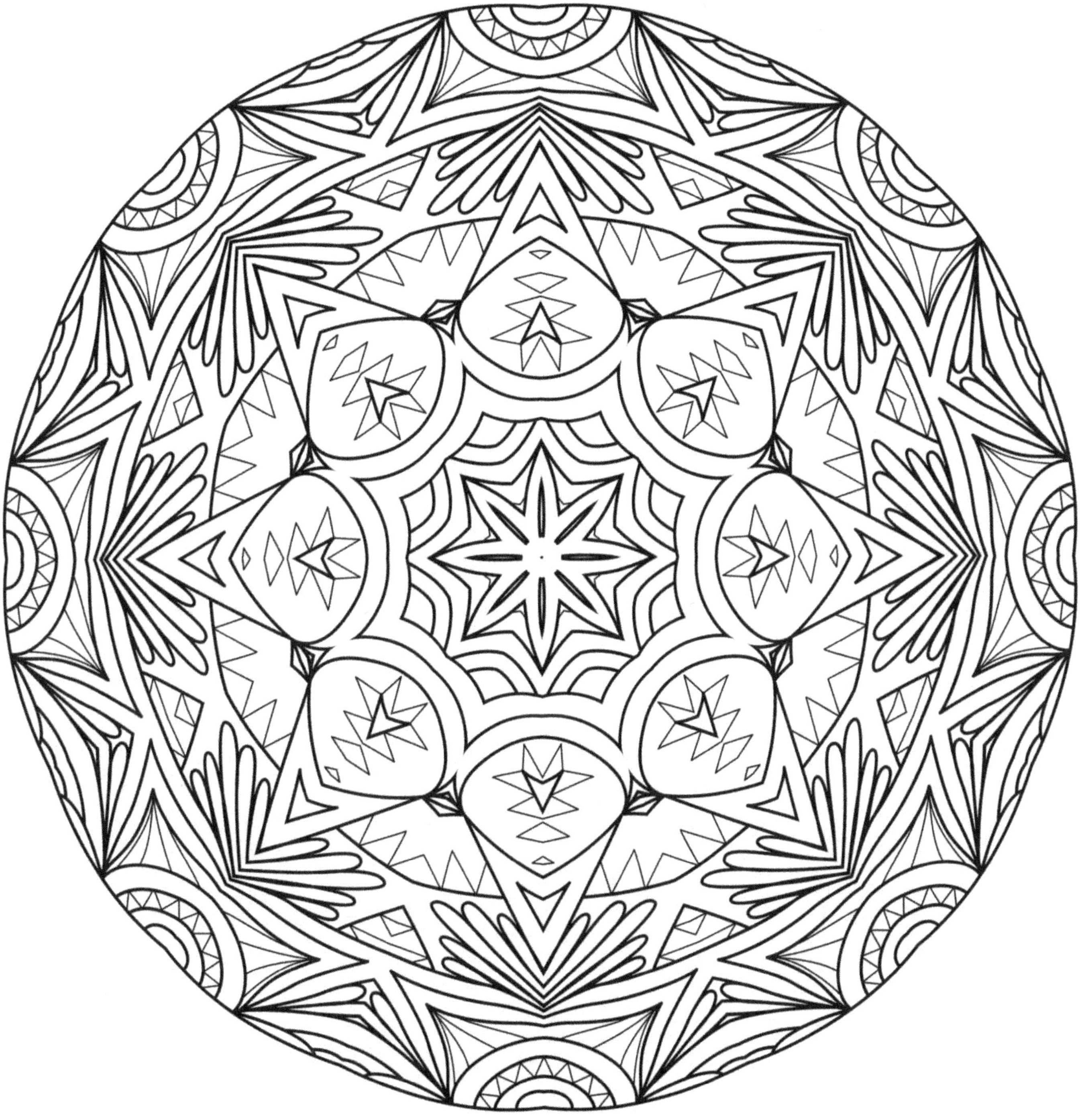

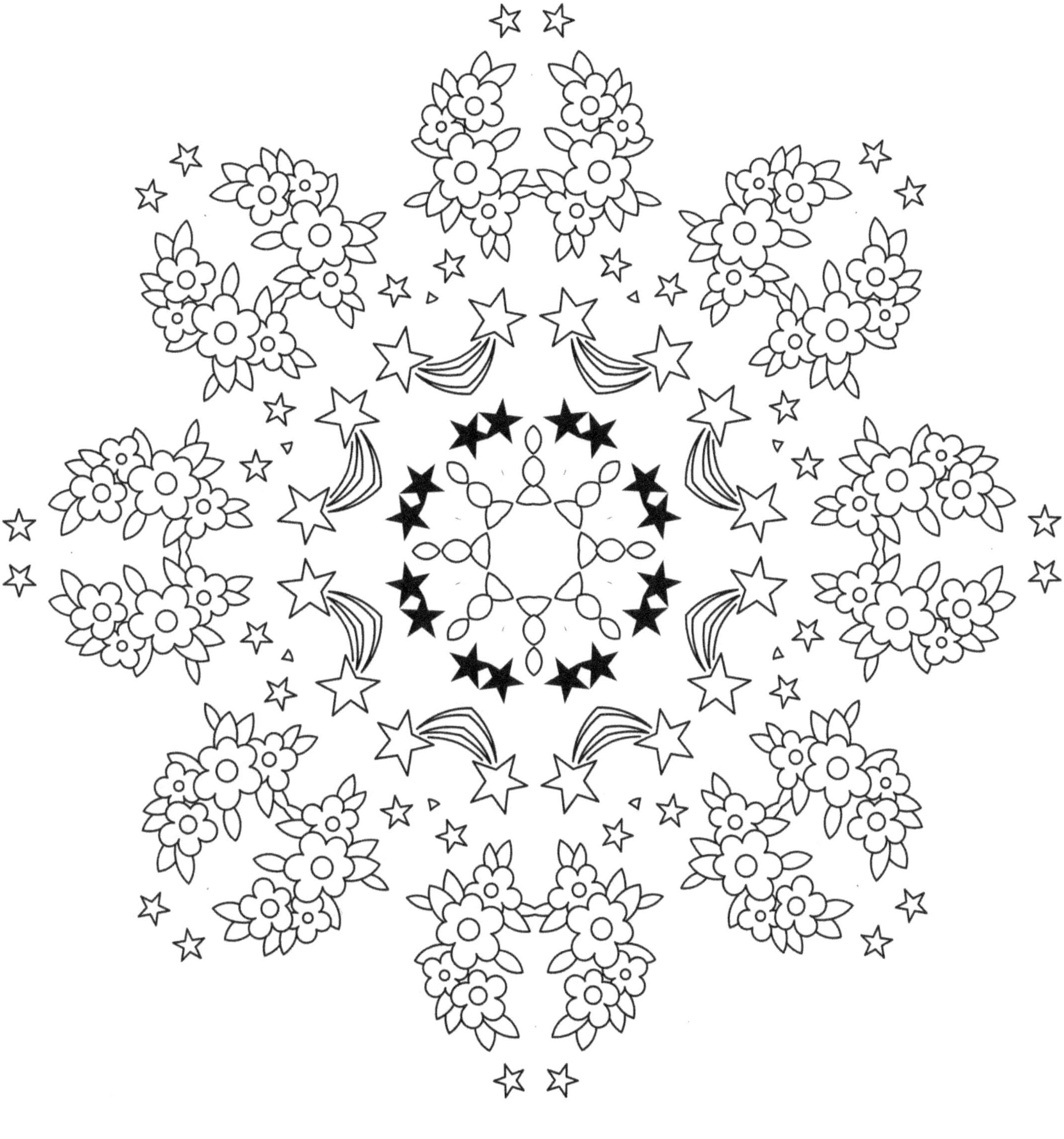

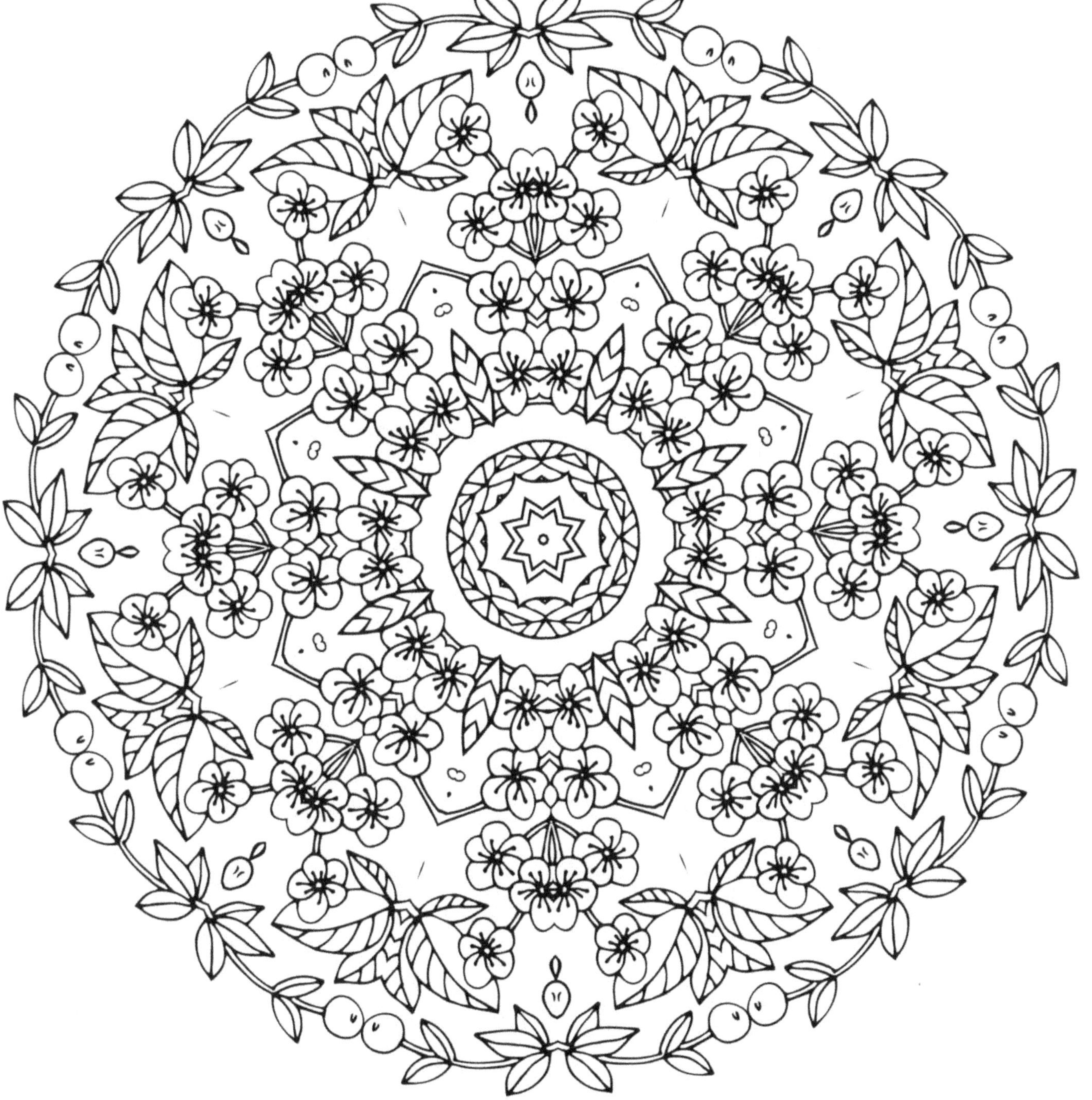

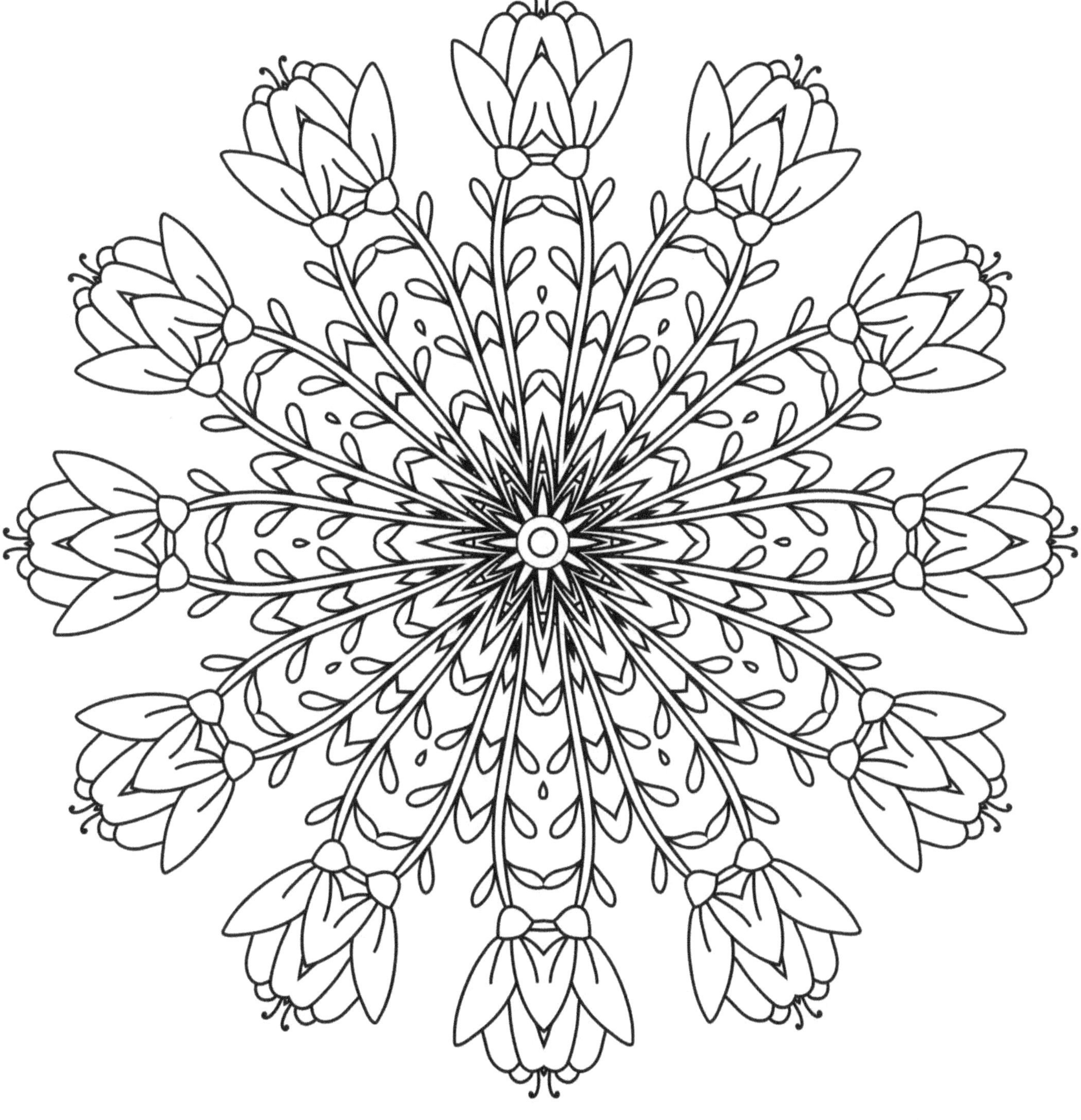

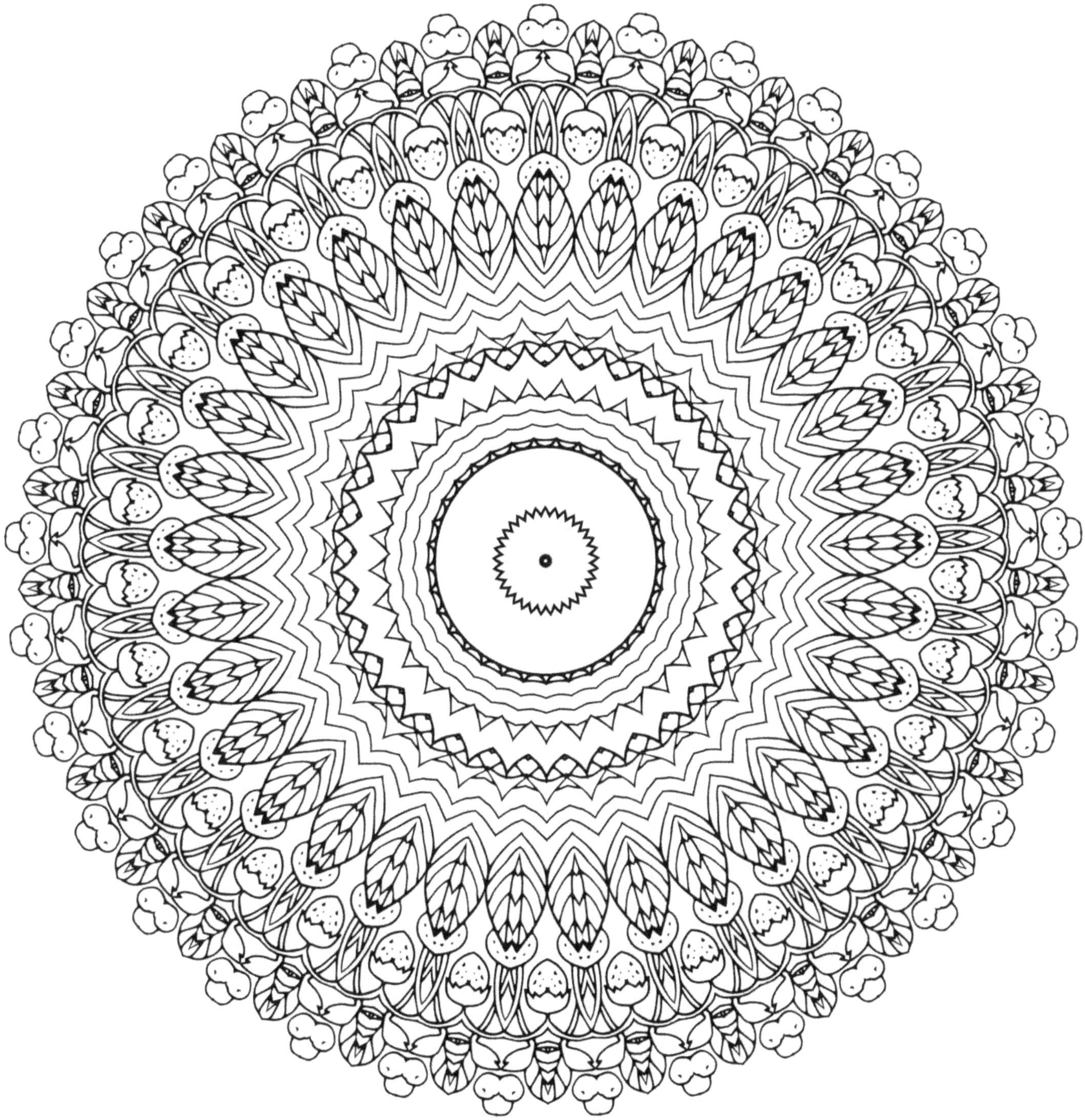

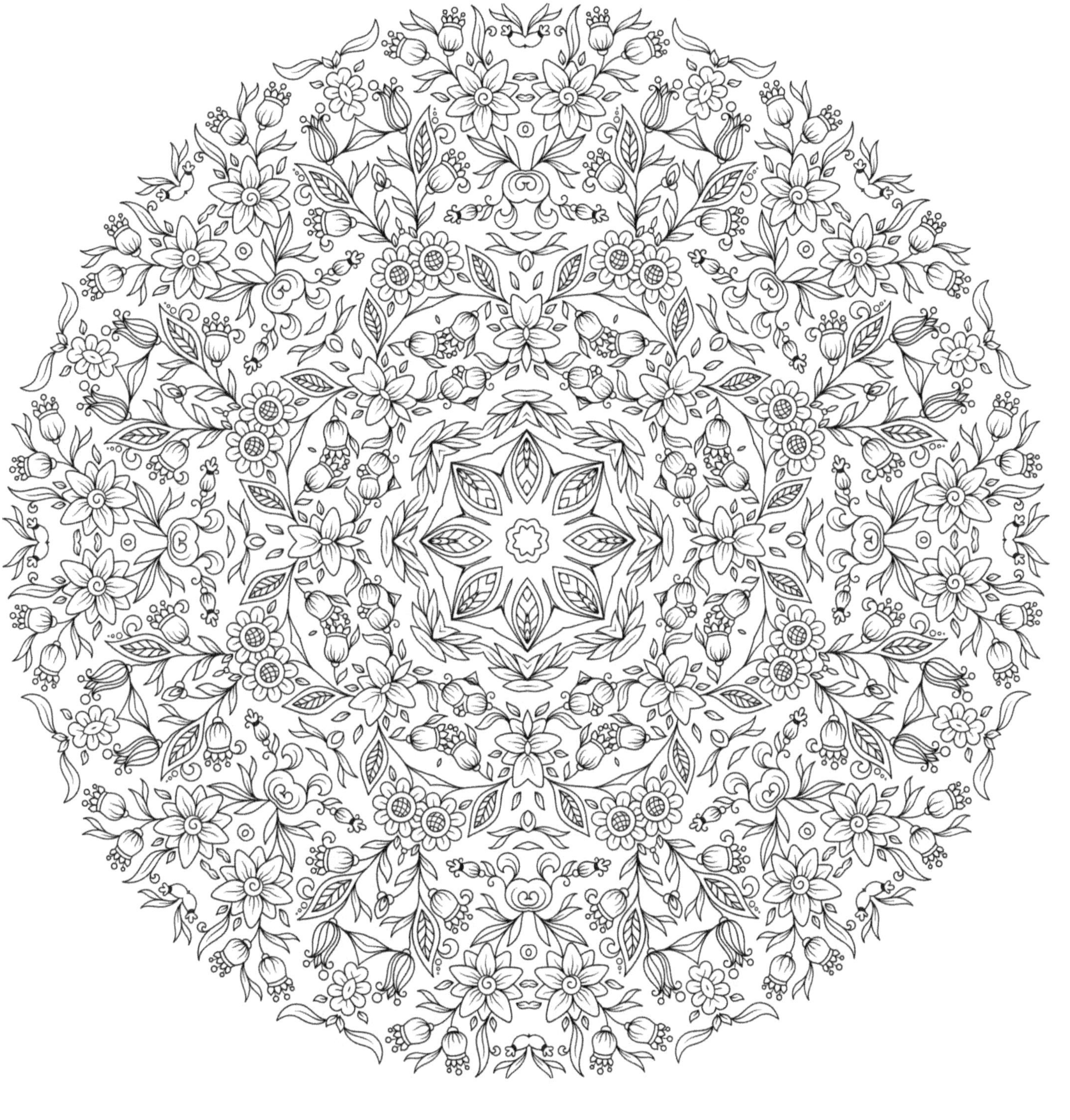

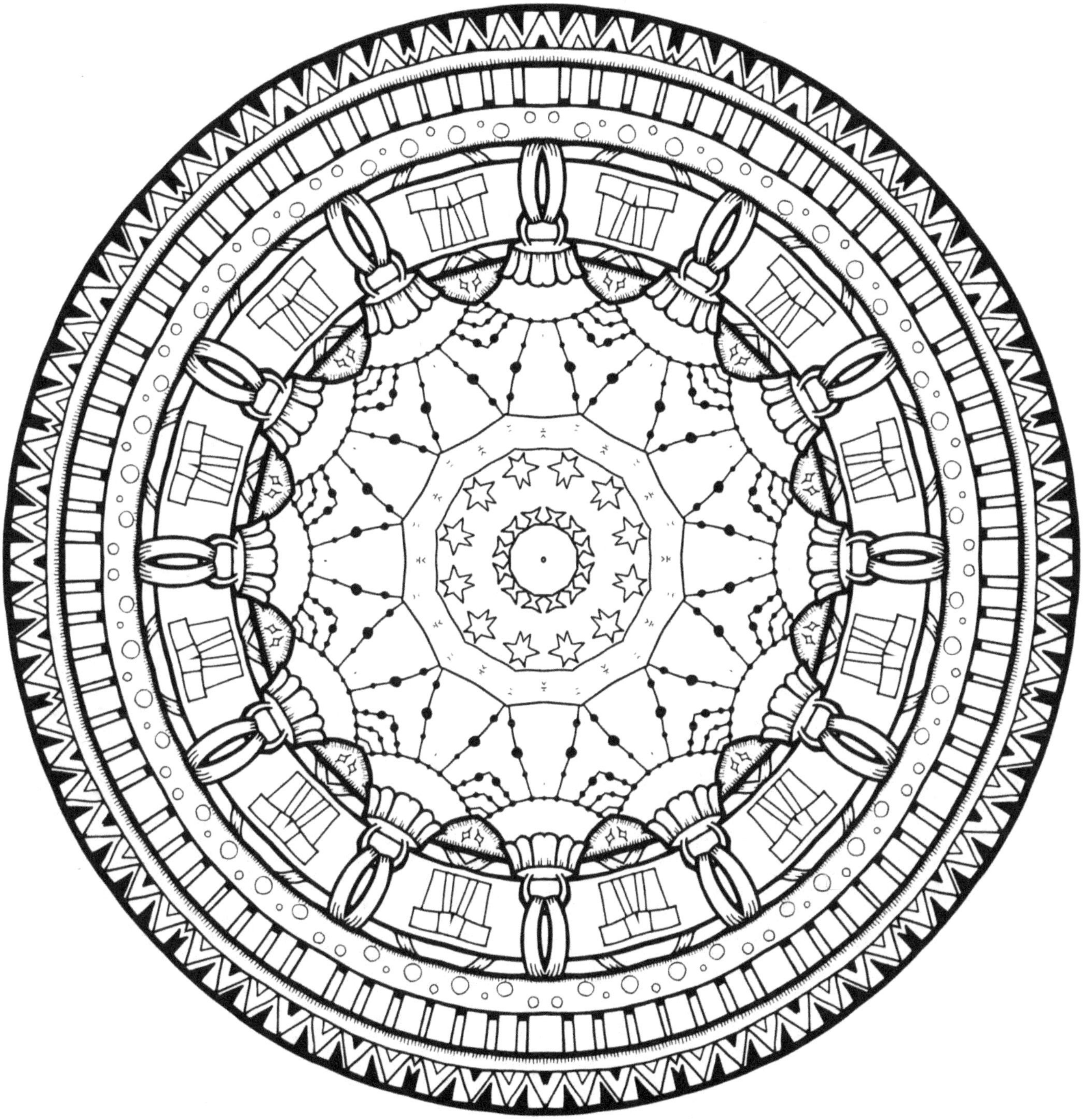

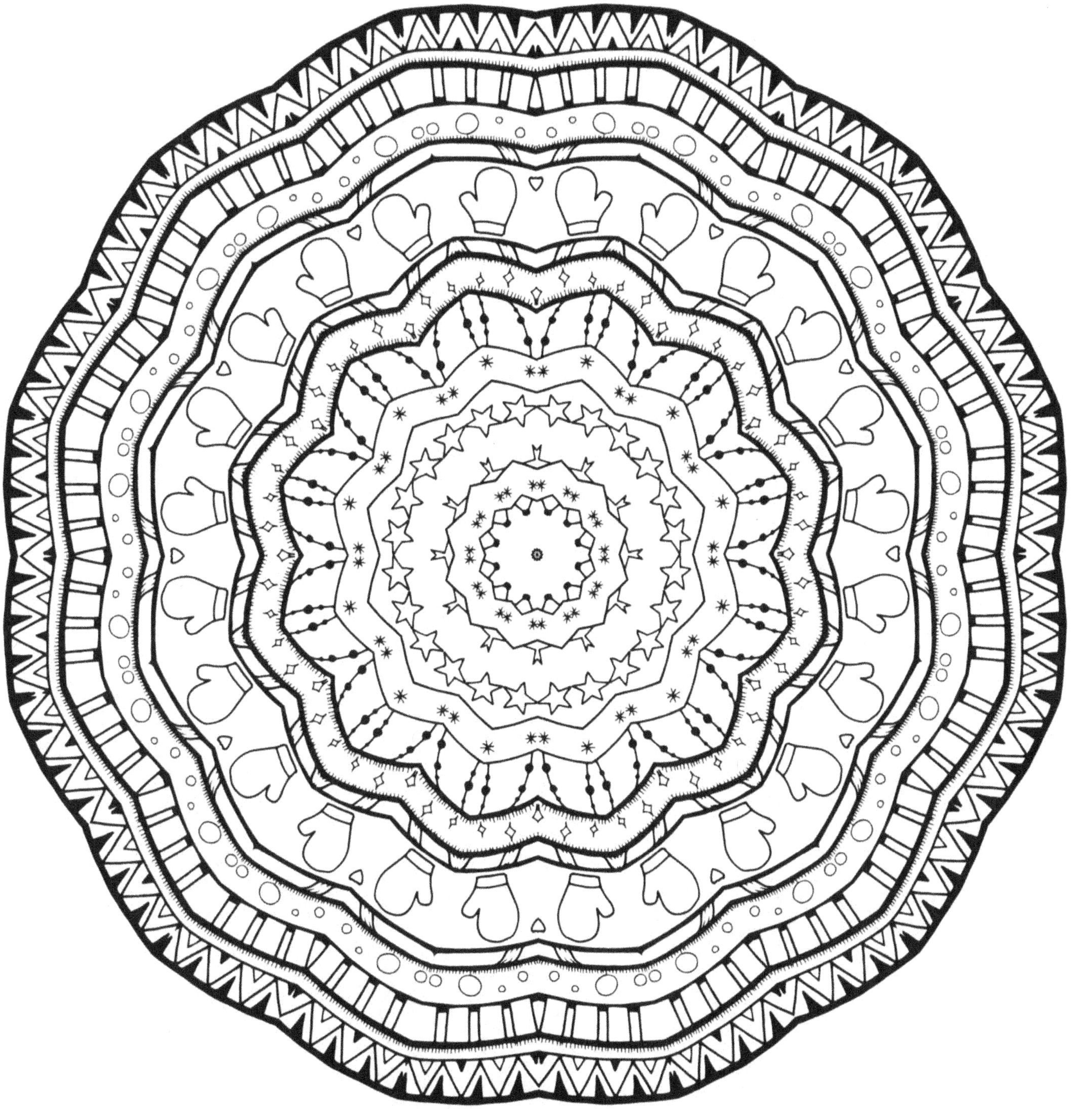

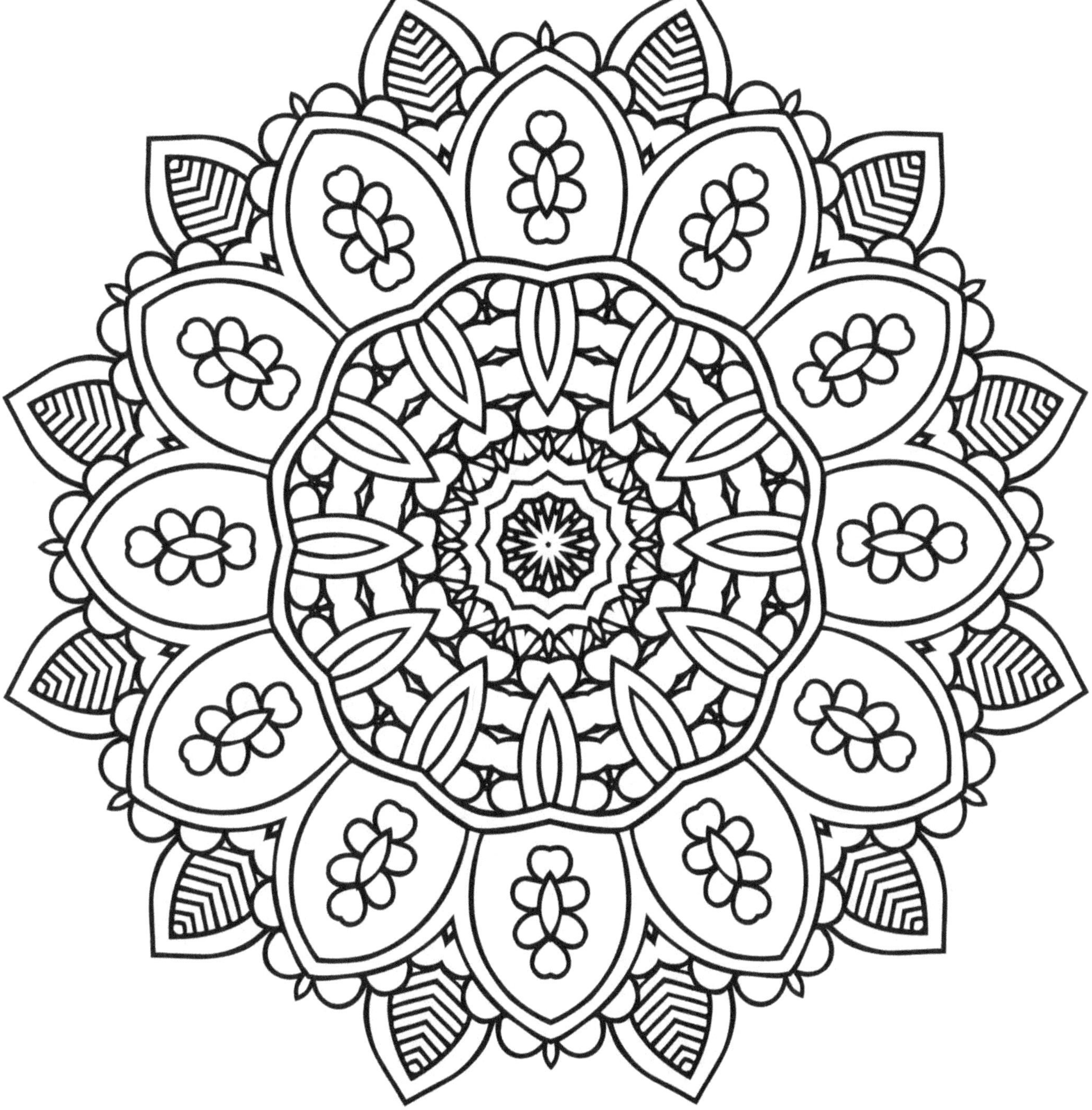

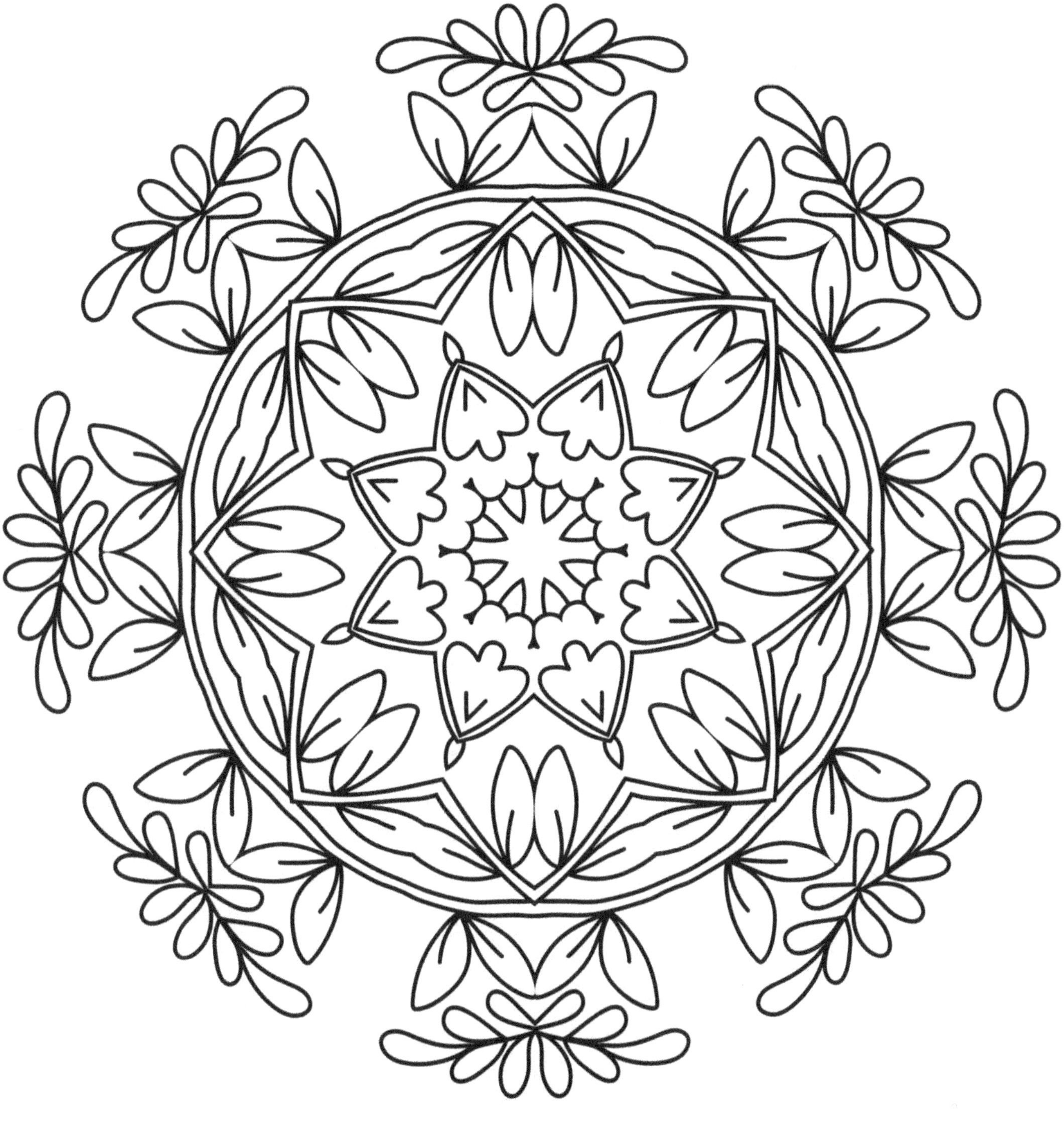

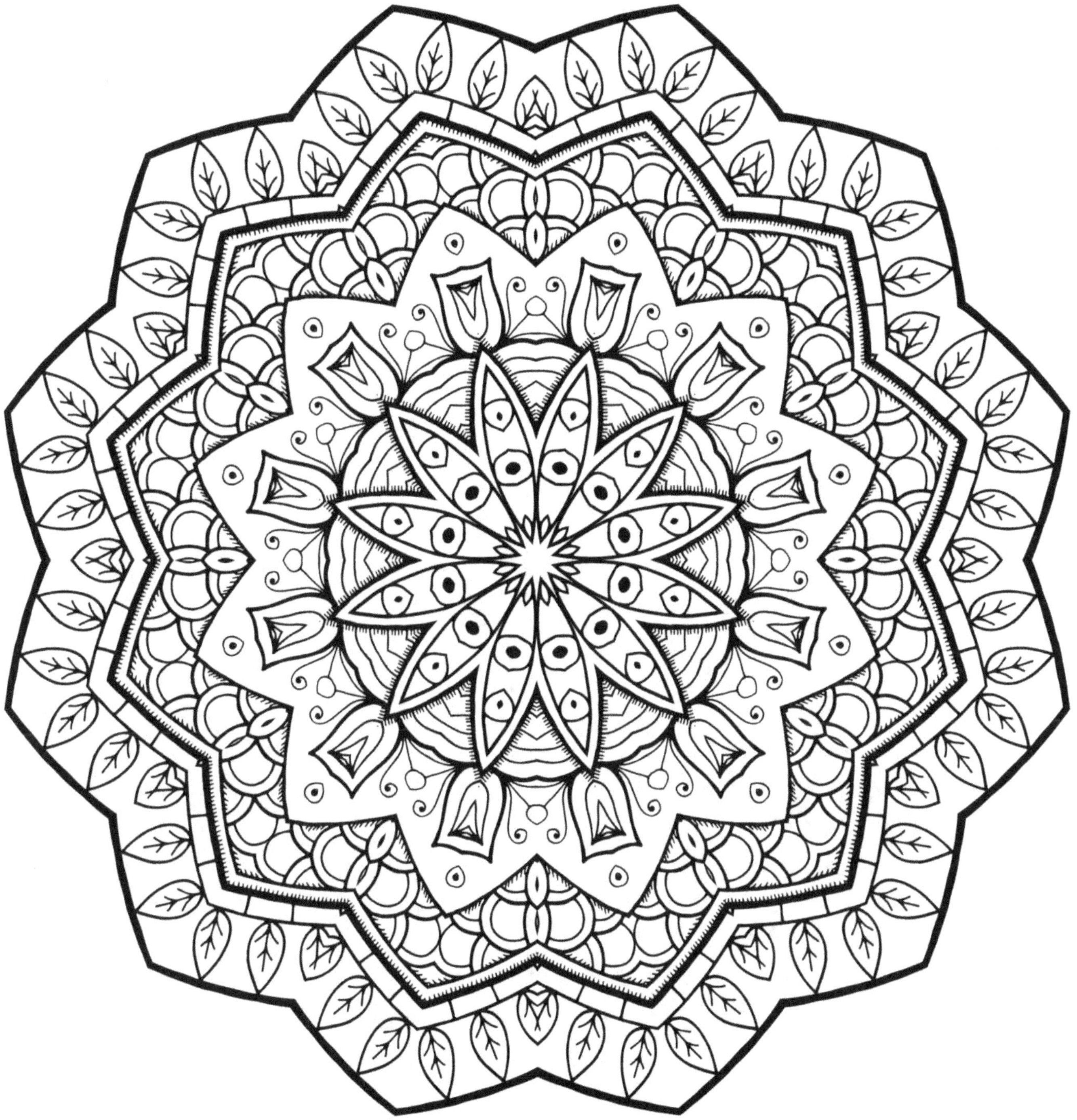

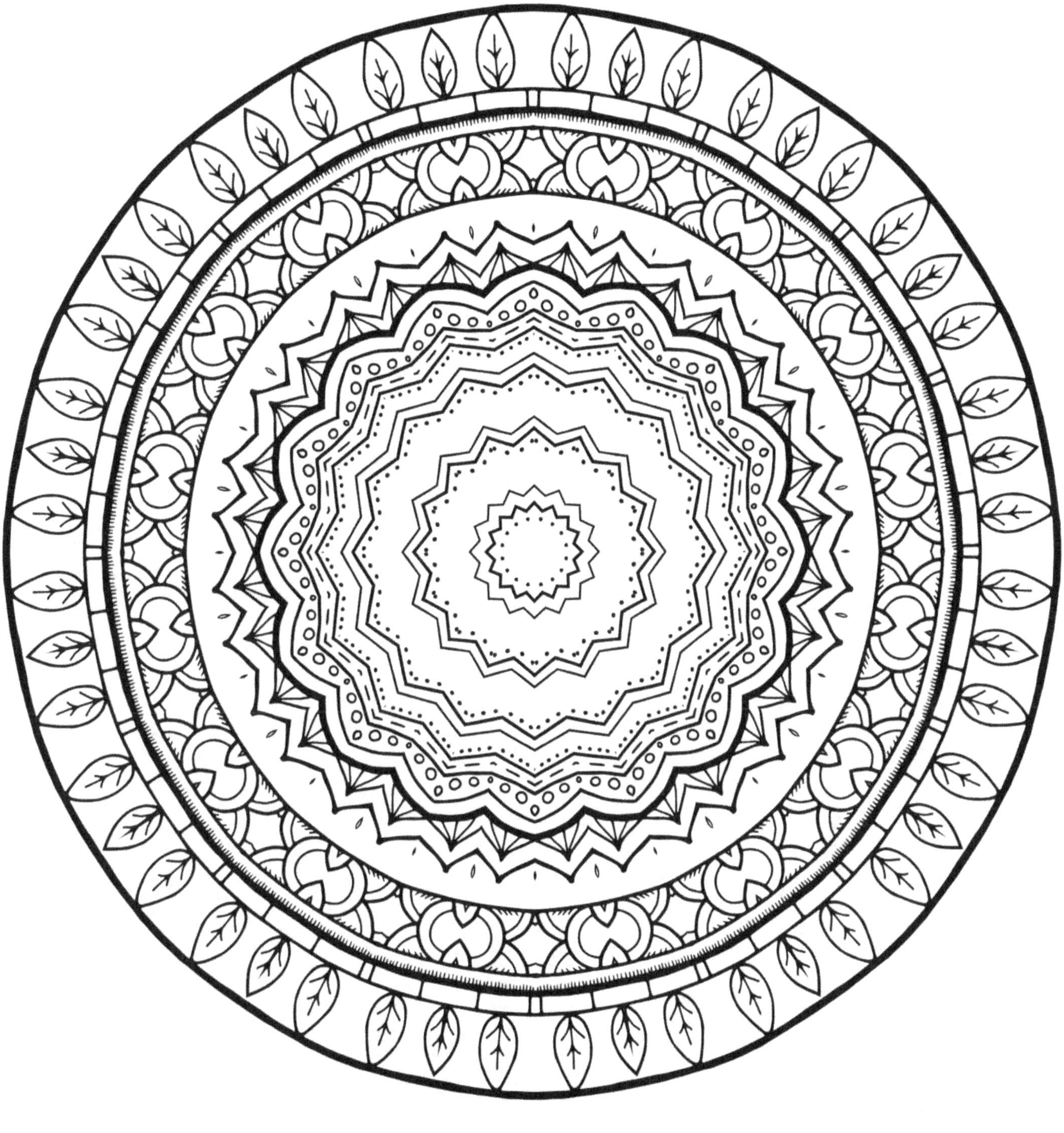

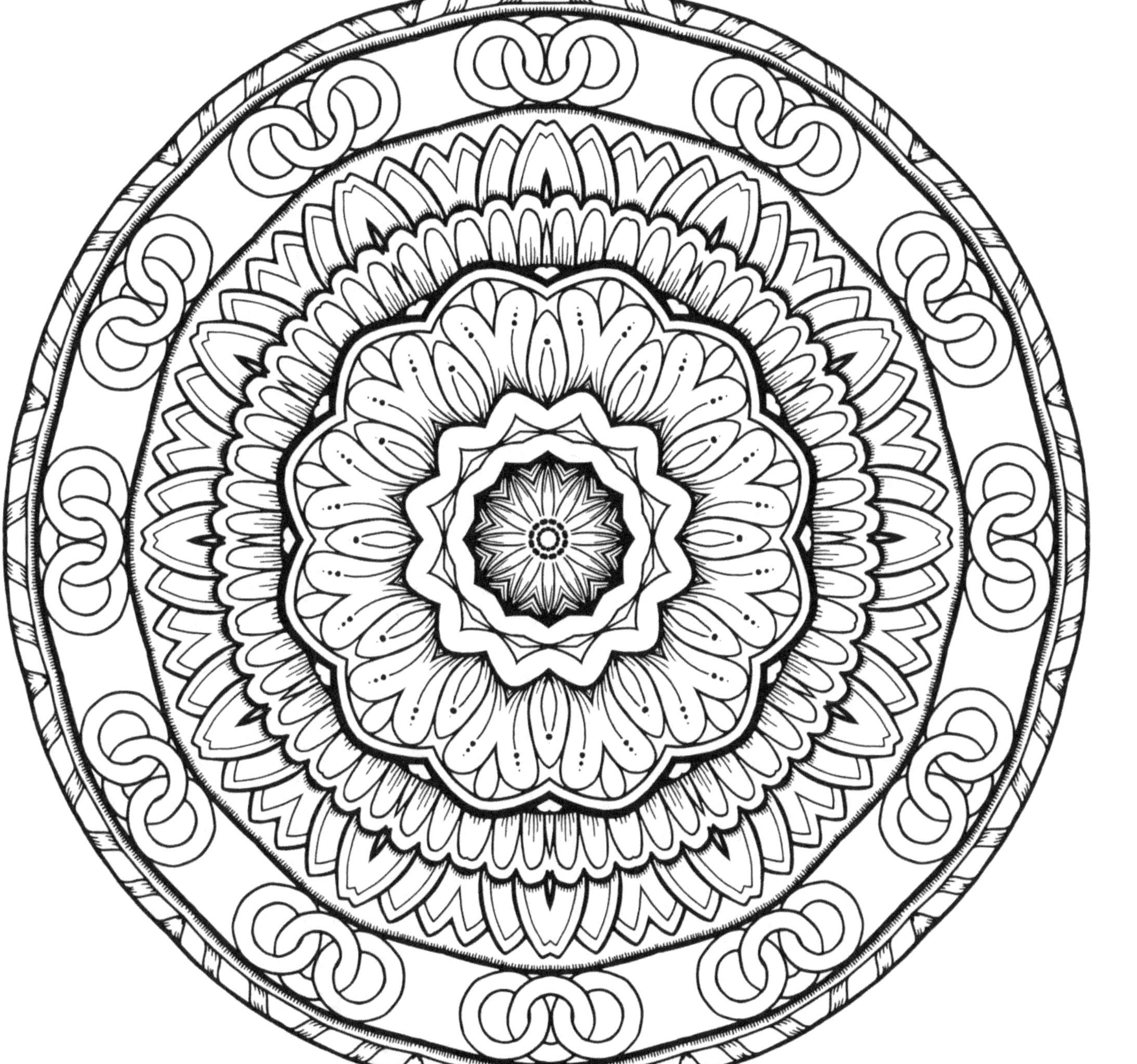

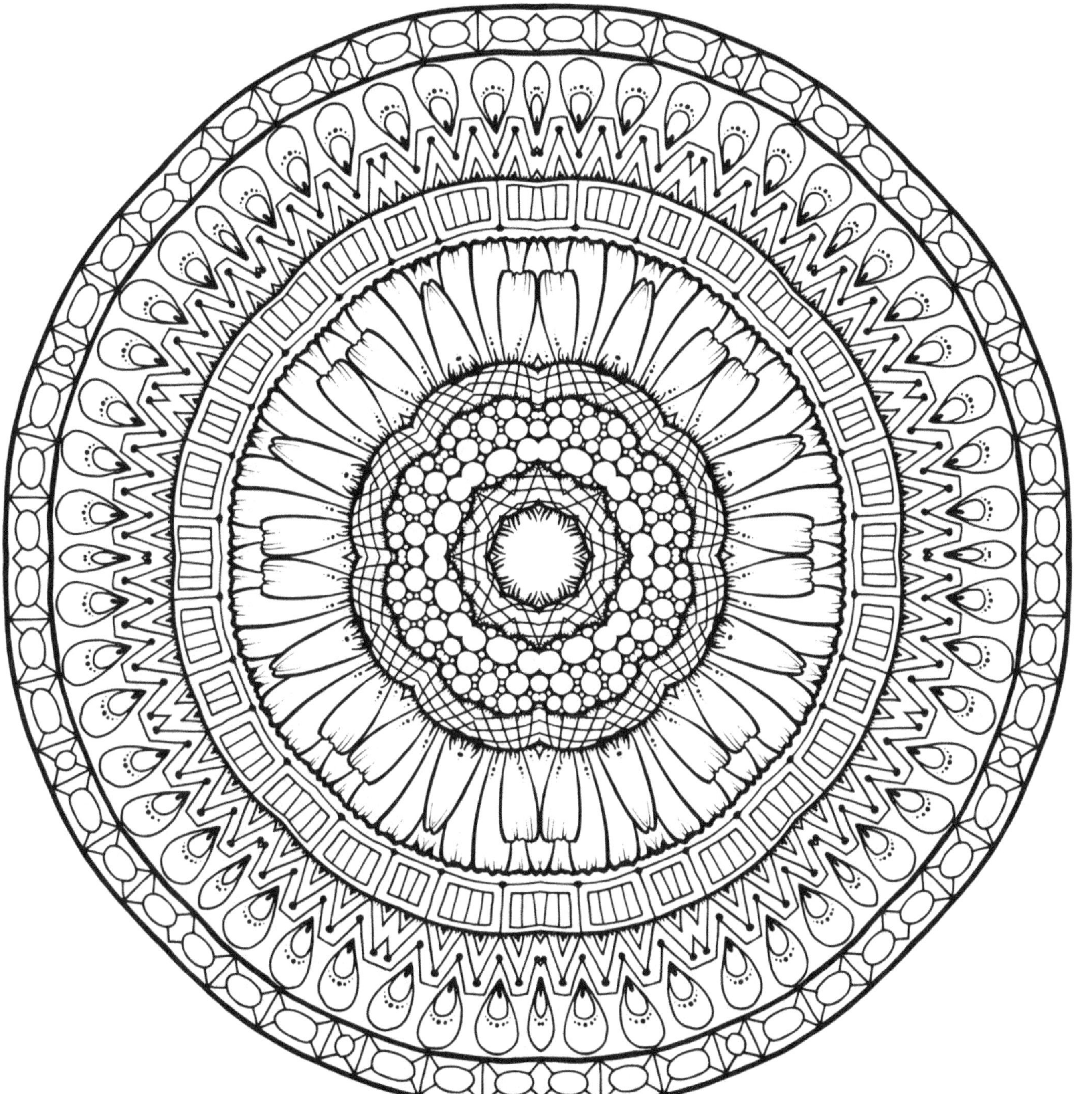

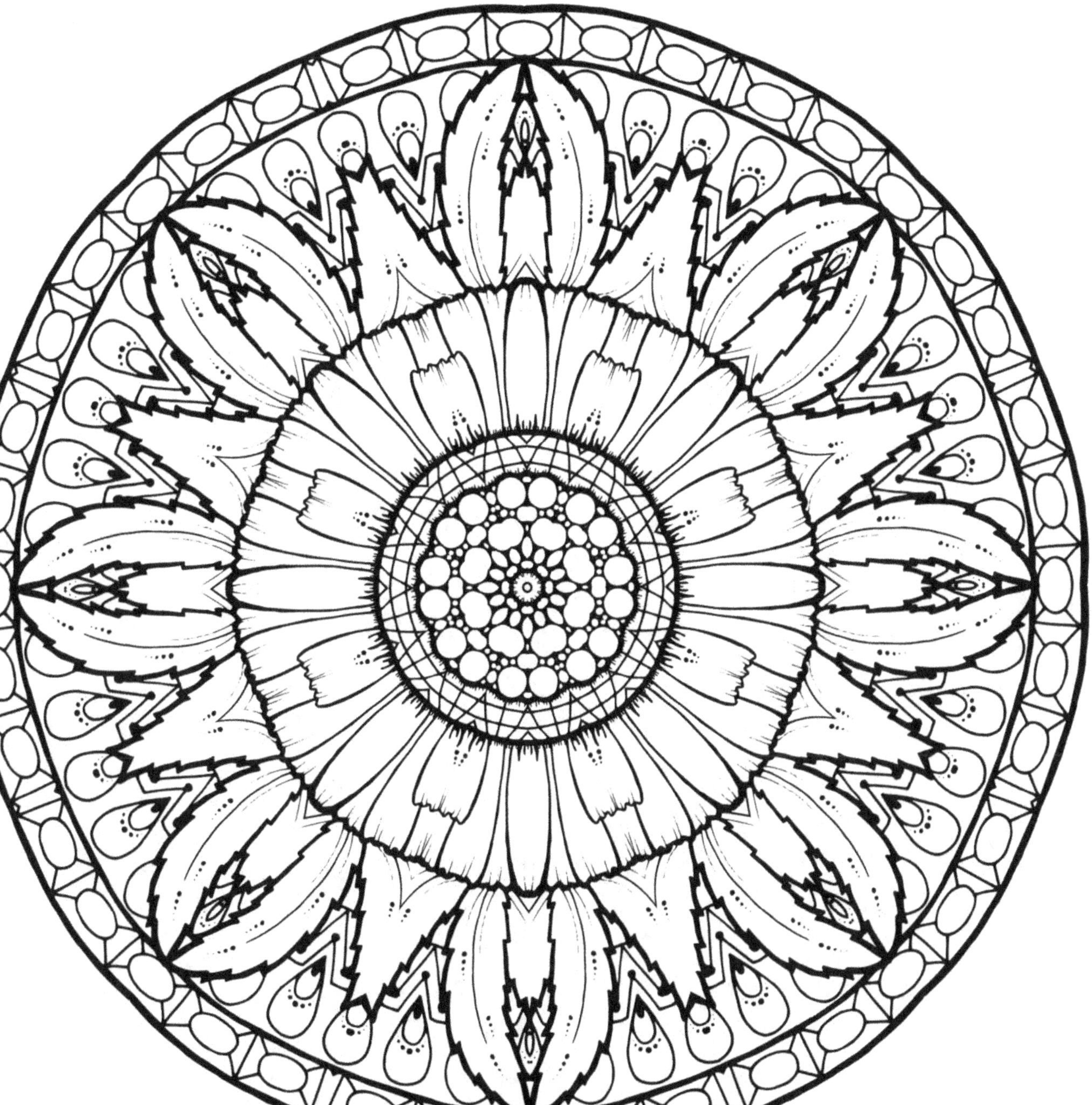

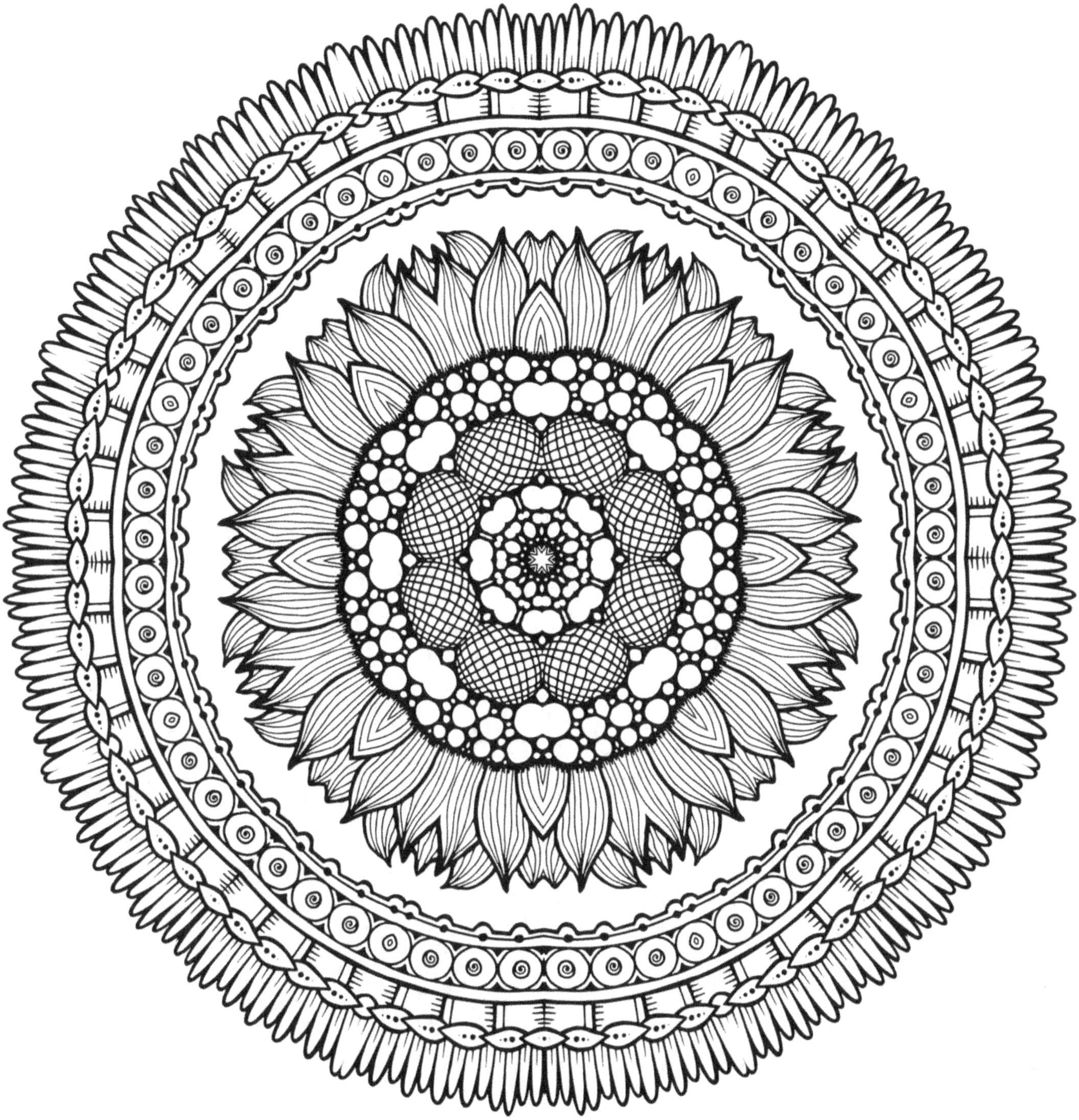

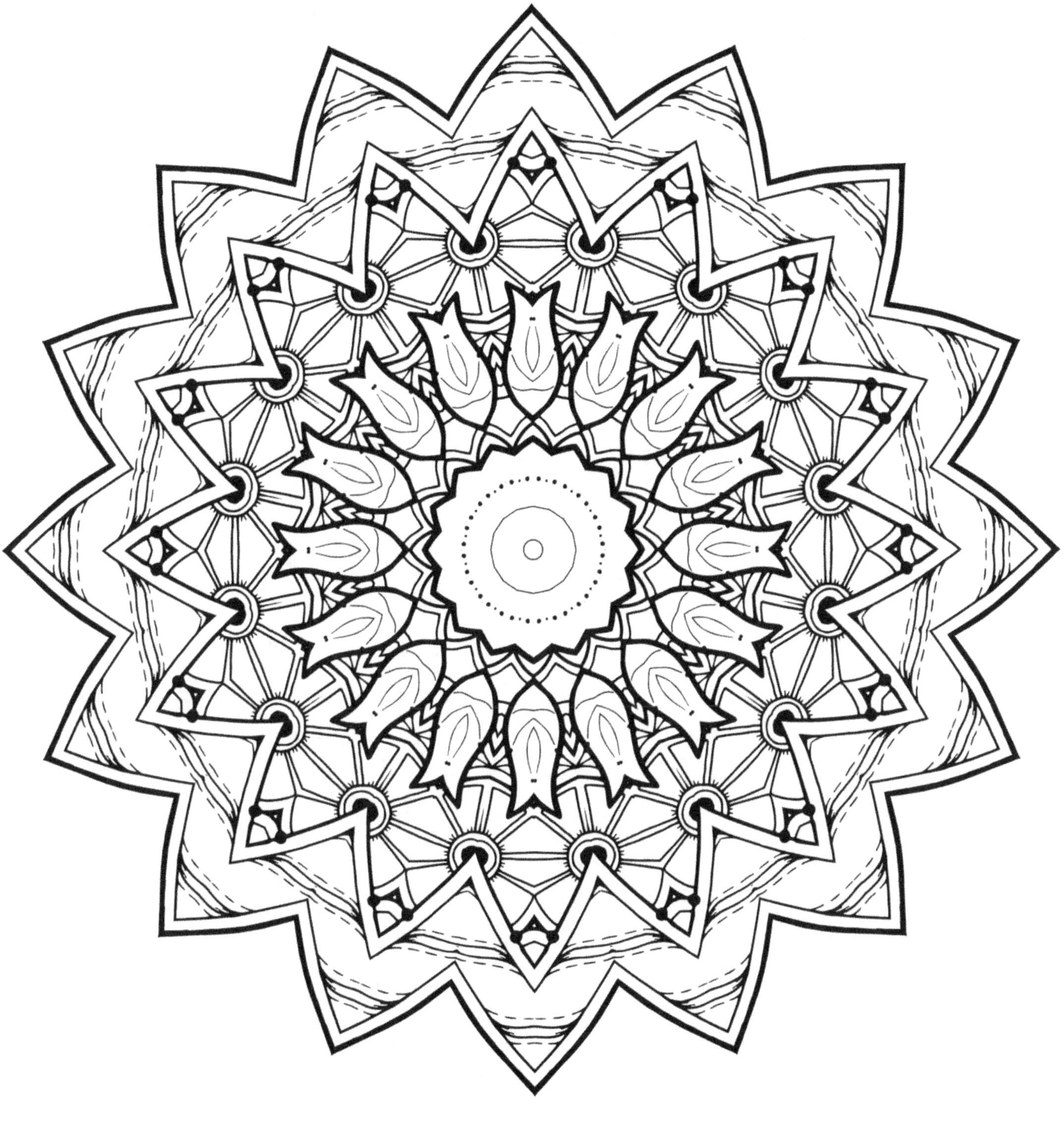

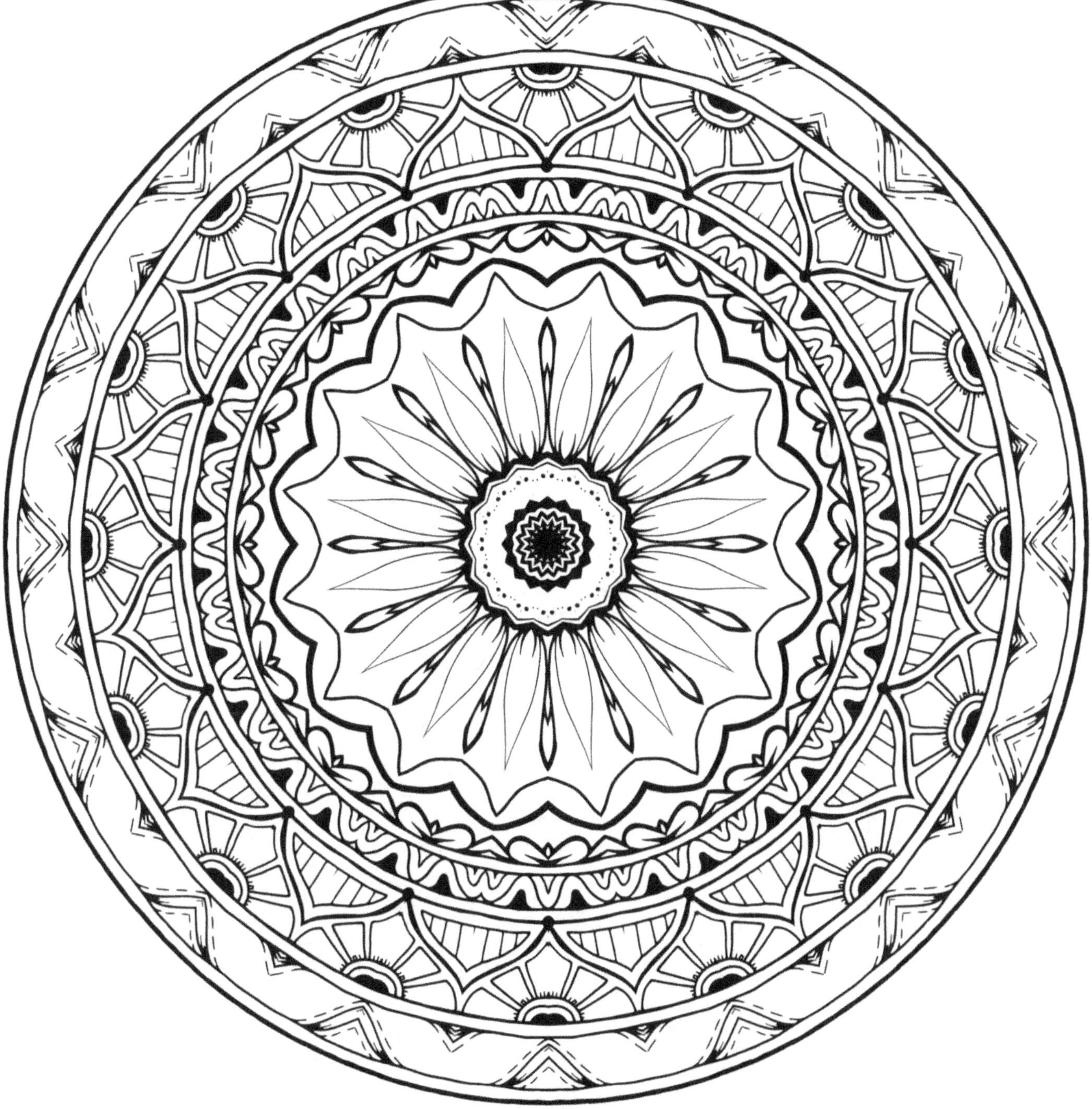

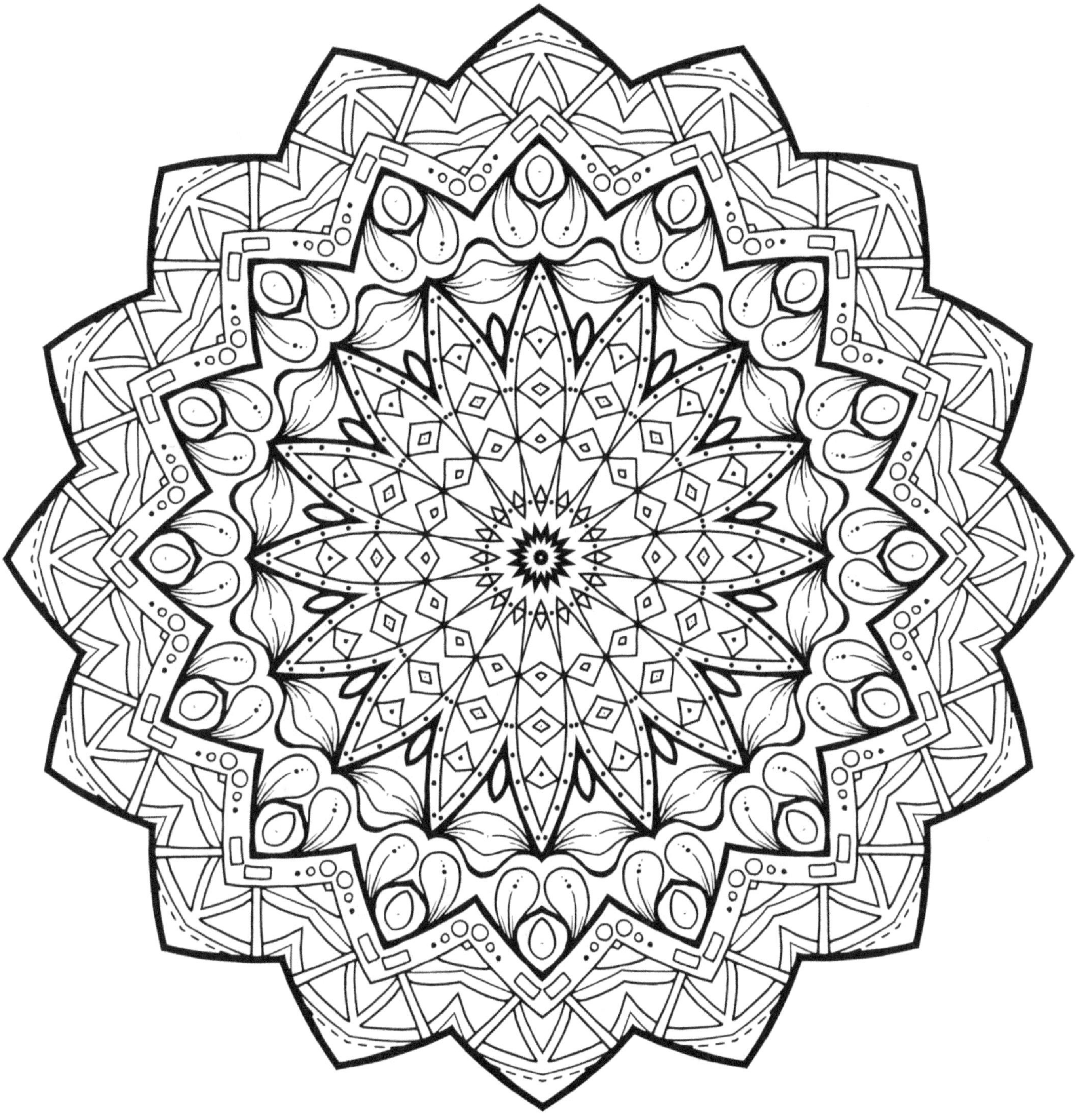

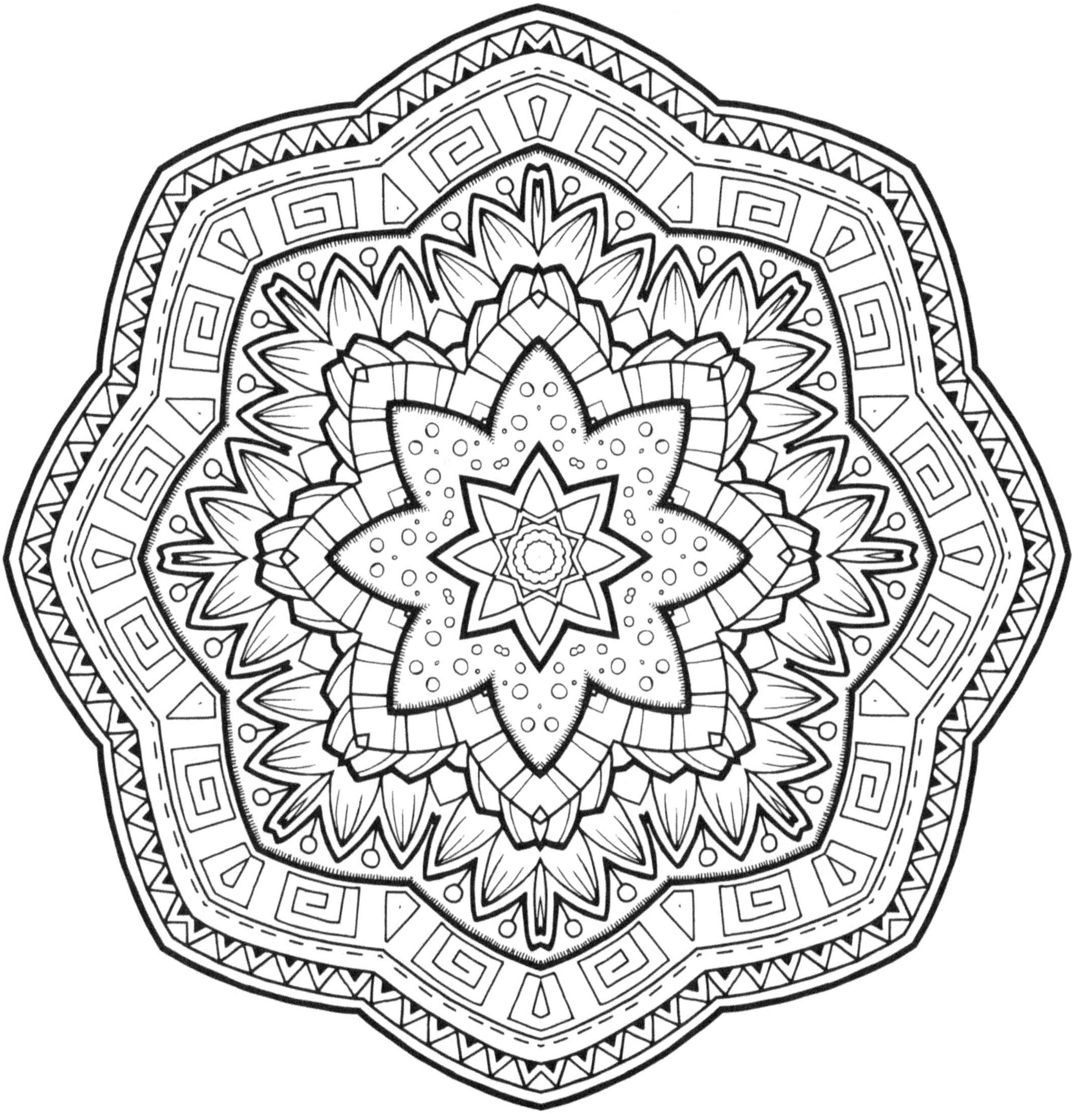

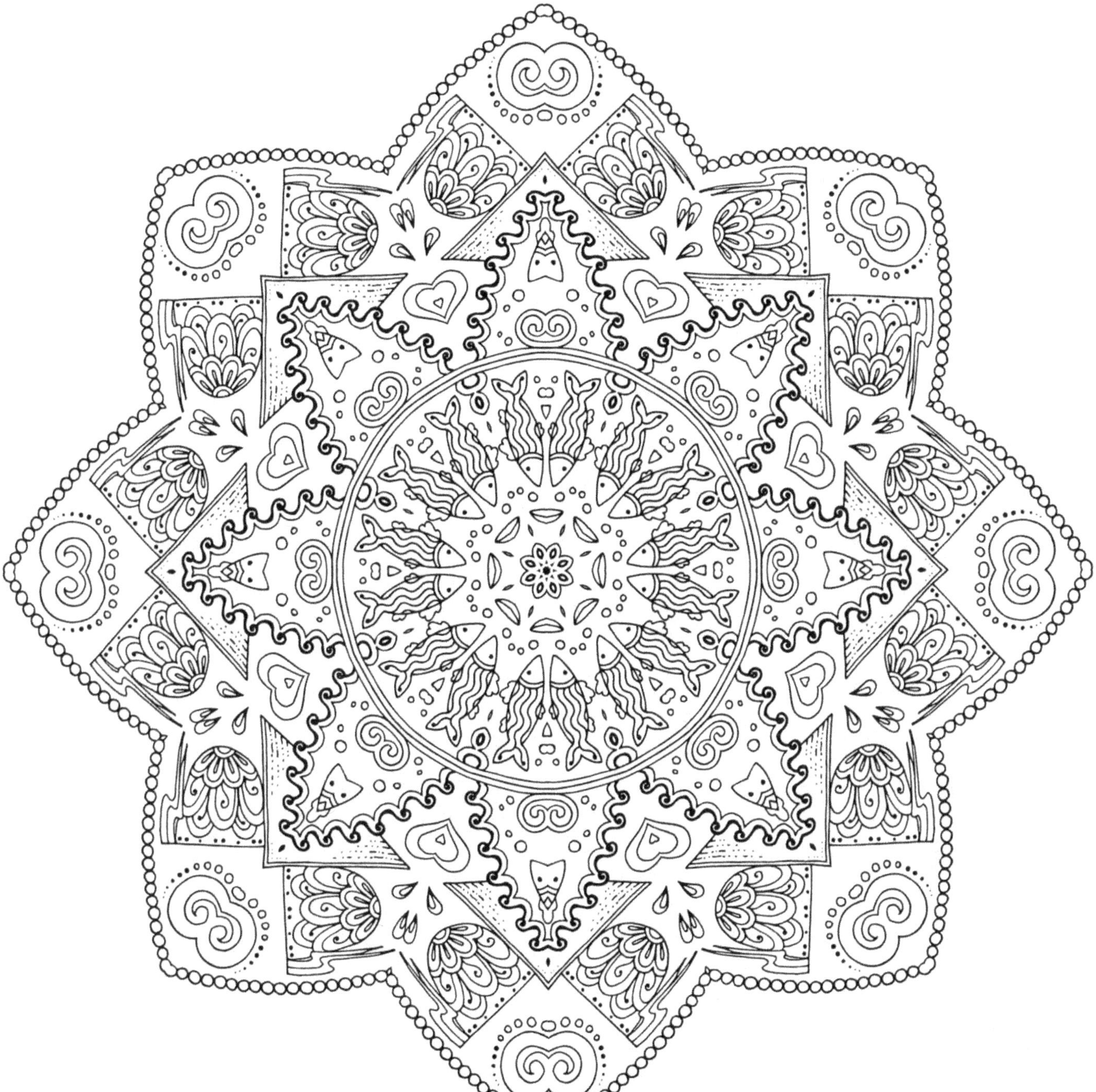

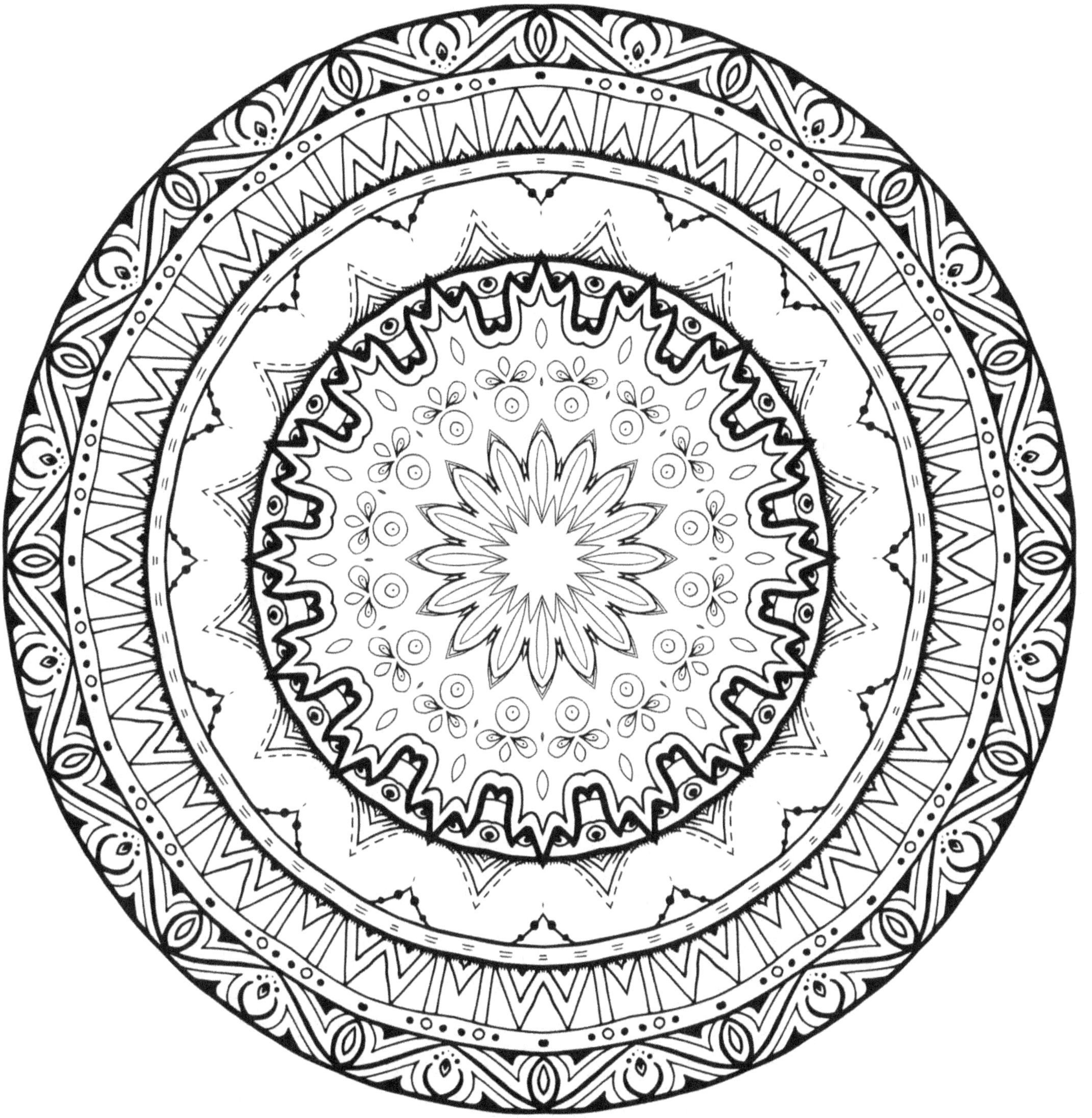

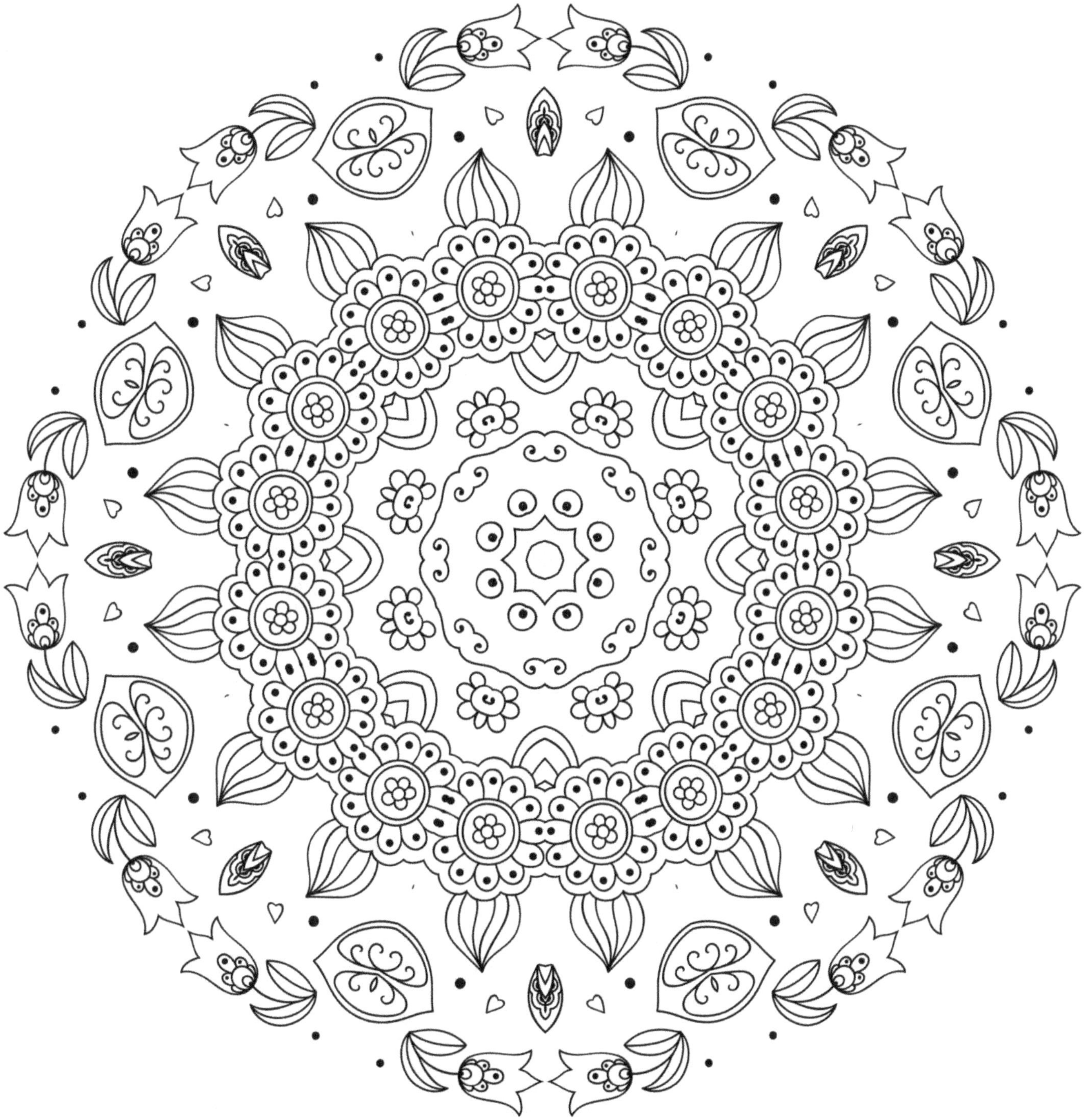

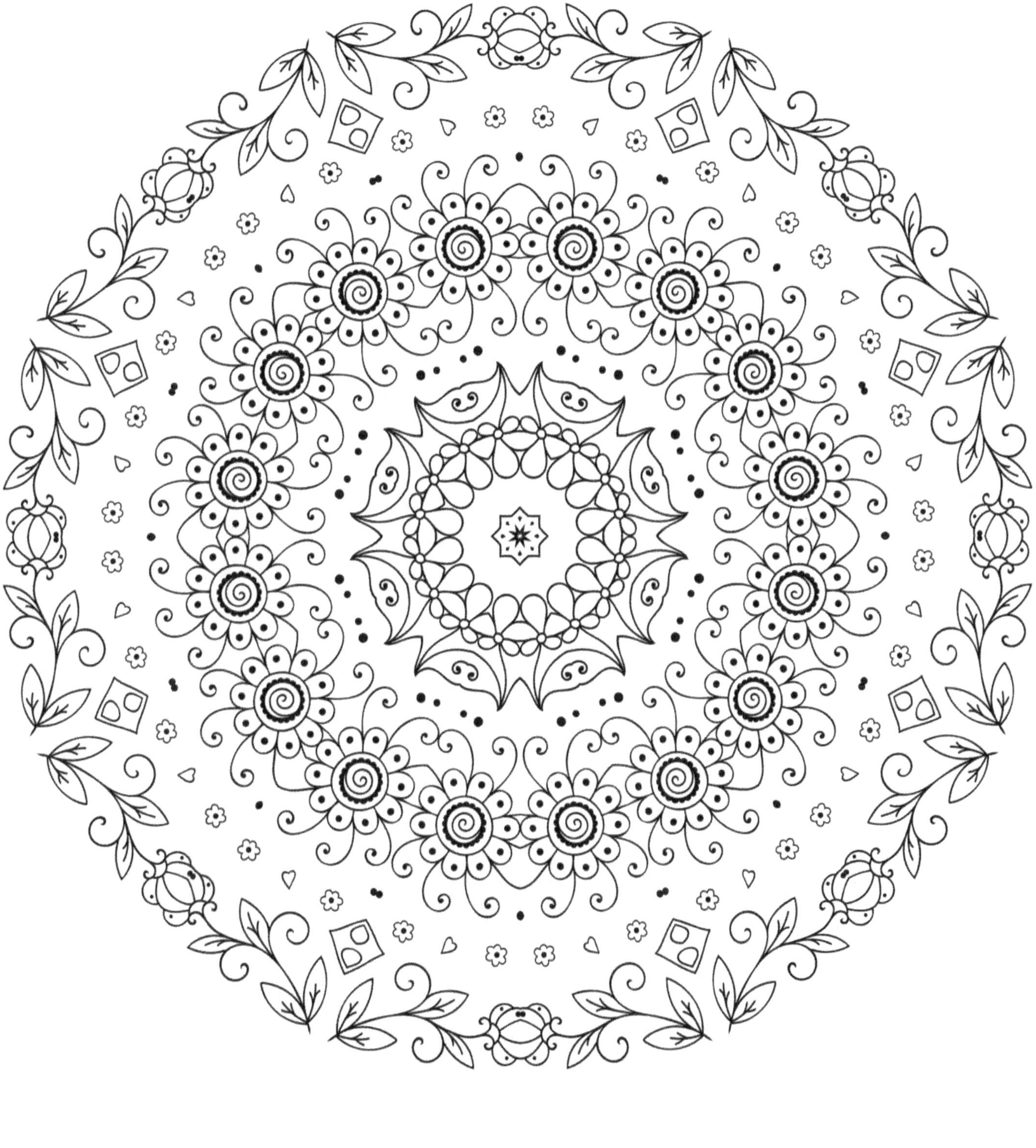

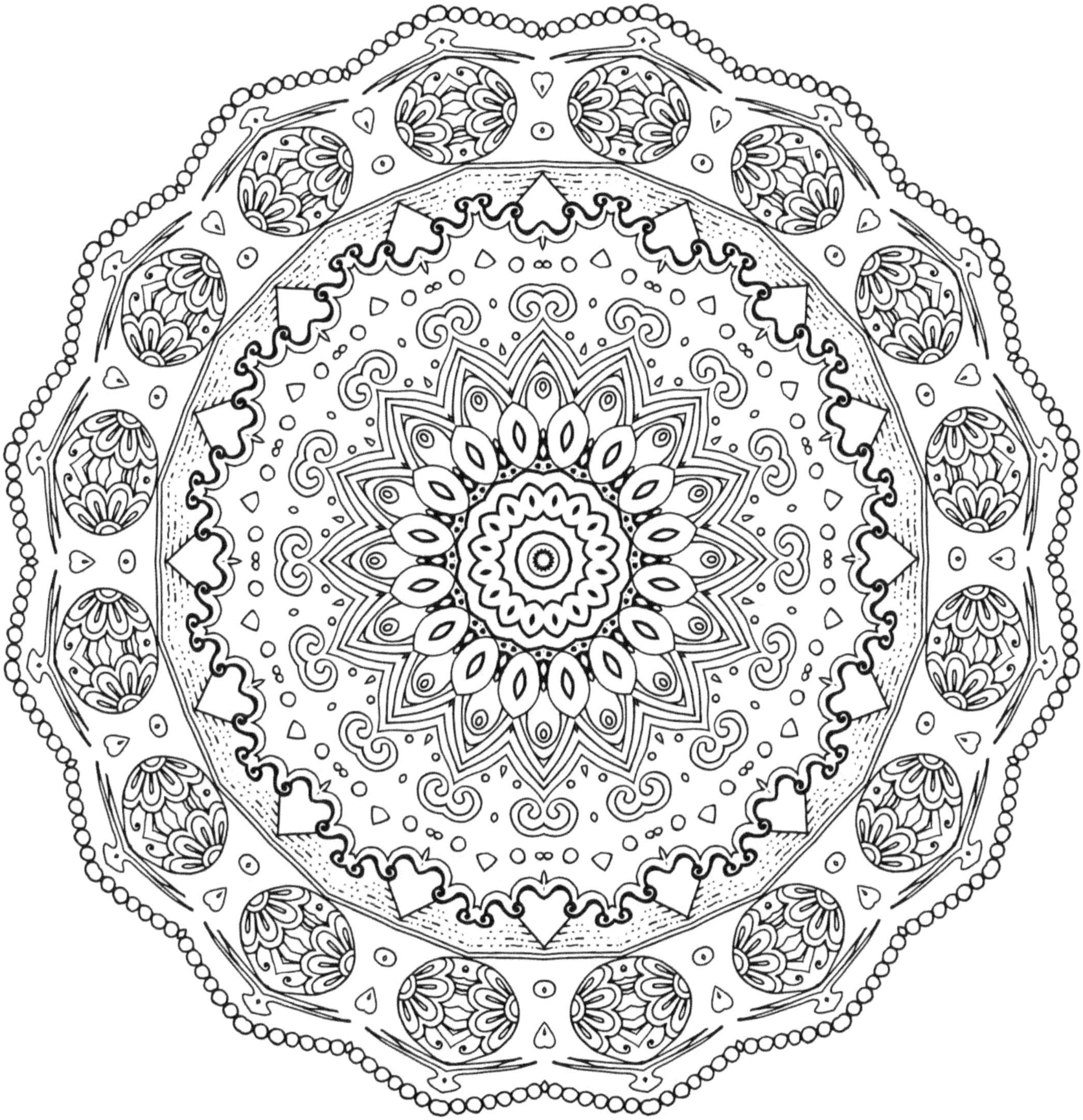

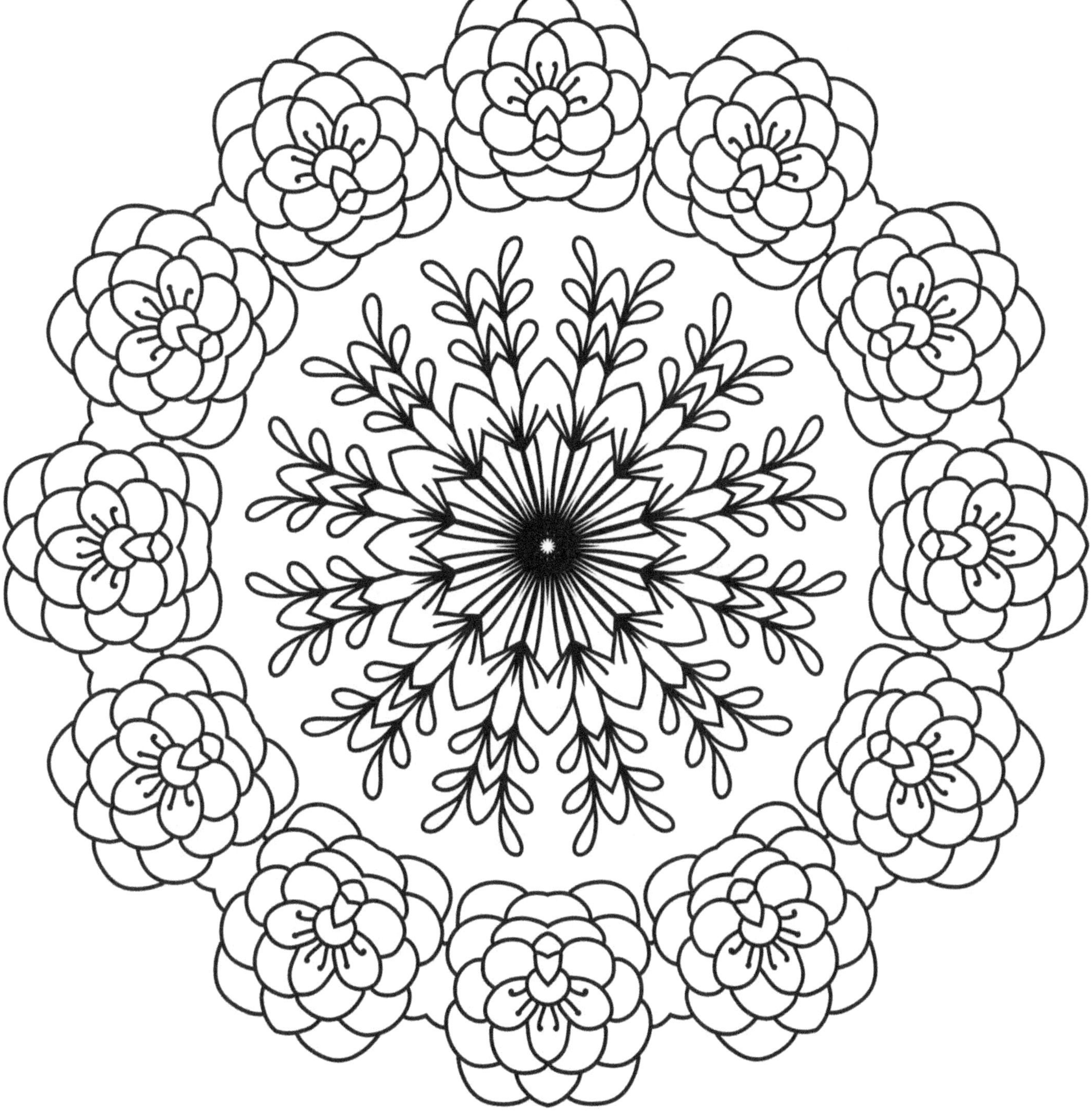

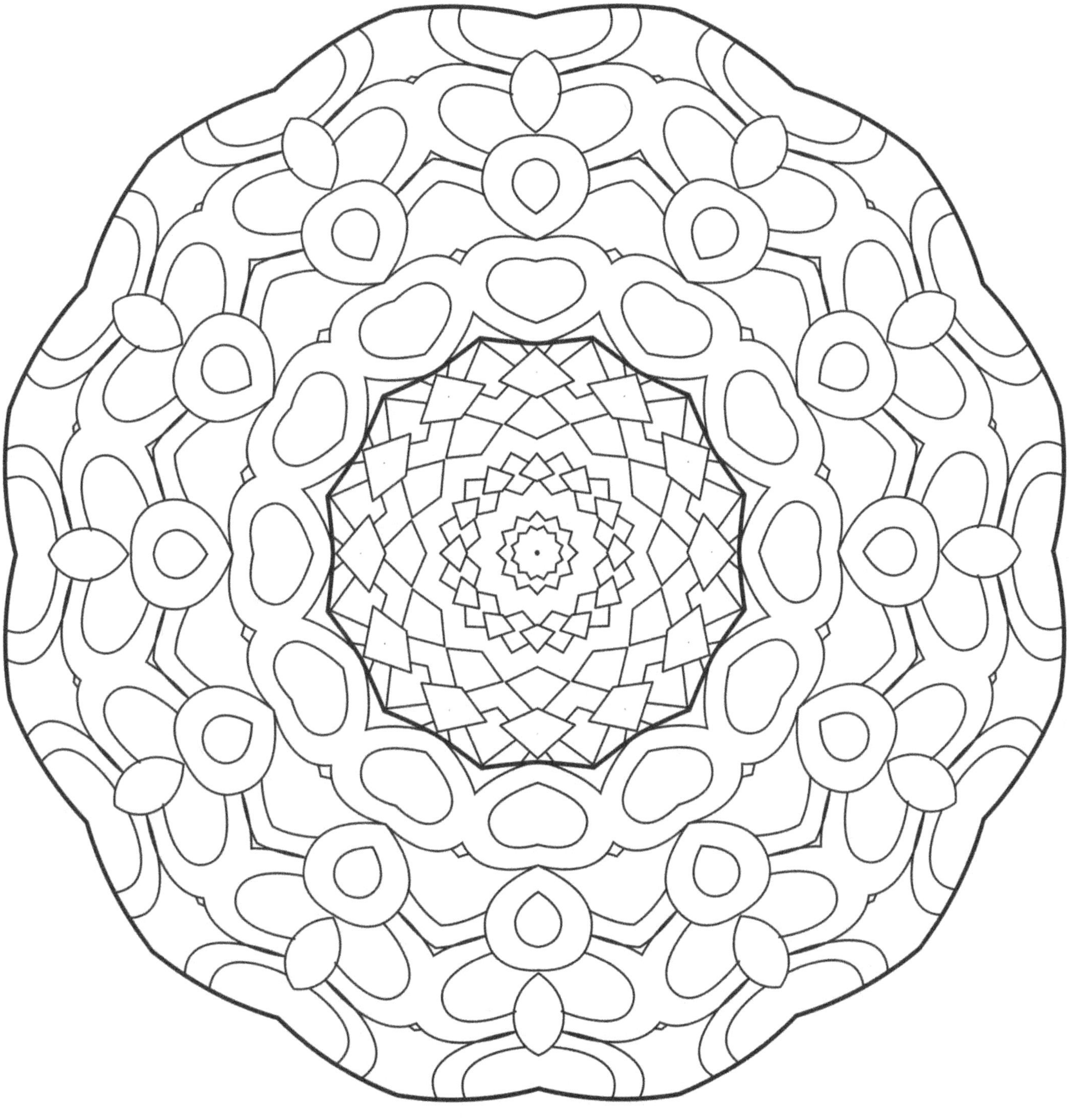

www.ingramcontent.com/pod-product-compliance
Lightning Source LLC
Chambersburg PA
CBHW081414280526
45788CB00009B/3101
* 9 7 8 1 5 4 4 7 4 2 8 8 5 *